INTERIORS
MIDWEST

leading designers
reveal their most
brilliant spaces

Published by

PANACHE
P A N A C H E   P A R T N E R S

Panache Partners, LLC
1424 Gables Court
Plano, TX 75075
469.246.6060
Fax: 469.246.6062
www.panache.com

Publishers: Brian G. Carabet and John A. Shand

Printed in Malaysia

Distributed by Independent Publishers Group
800.888.4741

PUBLISHER'S DATA

Interiors Midwest

Library of Congress Control Number: 2012953589

ISBN 13: 978-0-9886140-0-0
ISBN 10: 988614006

First Printing 2013

10 9 8 7 6 5 4 3 2 1

Right: Gooch Design Studio, page 176

Previous Page: Bardes Interiors, page 72

Panache Partners, LLC, is dedicated to the restoration and conservation
of the environment. Our books are manufactured with strict adherence
to an environmental management system in accordance with ISO
14001 standards, including the use of paper from mills certified to
derive their products from well-managed forests. We are committed
to continued investigation of alternative paper products and
environmentally responsible manufacturing processes to ensure the
preservation of our fragile planet.

INTERIORS
MIDWEST

introduction

Reddington Designs, page 190

Jenna Wedemeyer Design, page 106

Simultaneously exhilarating and formidable, the process of interior design is unlike any other undertaking. To extract the essence that will reflect those living within the home, designers must embark on a journey through the homeowner's life. The process requires knowledge of multiple disciplines, enthusiasm to persevere over time, and a keen ability to understand and communicate with a plethora of personalities.

Taking into account contrasting principles at work in each home, designers pour their energy into transforming imagination into reality. Ensuring that each room has a flavor of its own as part of a cohesive overall design and that each room is relevant to modern life with a timelessness that can't be denied, designers fashion spaces to be private sanctuaries for families and entertaining spaces for guests.

Interiors Midwest features the impressive work of professionals who effortlessly meet all the challenges of design, expressing the homeowner's lifestyle and sense of style in ways never before imagined. This book lays the foundation for inspiration through unparalleled images that present an insider's look into private retreats, and delves even deeper as the experts reveal their philosophies and advice gleaned through years of experience.

Within this extraordinary collection, you'll find cozy waterside retreats, high-rise condos with sweeping views of Chicago, suburban estates reimagined for the 21st century, and weekend cottages that beckon relaxation from everyday life. From Green Bay to the Great Lakes, traditional suburban abodes to contemporary urban dwellings, these designers passionately redefine what it means to turn a house into a home.

contents

Dazzling Designs, page 28

Bryan Bilczewski Design, page 18

Bardes Interiors

Passionate about design and renovation from childhood, Cindy Bardes Galvin seemed destined to beautify homes. Earning her interior design degree from Northwestern University, Cindy worked for a design firm for a few years before founding Bardes Interiors. Inspired by European aesthetics and couture fashions, Cindy combines color, texture, and pattern to give traditional designs a modern twist. Classic influences and natural materials are ever-present elements in spaces touched by her creativity. She approaches every project with the goal of creating harmonious, livable spaces for homeowners and her word-of-mouth success stands as testimony of that achievement. In December of 2009, Cindy opened MAZE Home Store, conveniently located for Chicago's North Shore shoppers. Now the home of Bardes Interiors, MAZE is just another way Cindy brings fine design to all.

Above & Facing Page: Pulling the outside in is something I try to do in every room I design. In a home that is flooded with light—with floor-to-ceiling windows on many walls—I brought together a combination of soothing wood tones with blues and greens to create a calm atmosphere. White oak floors with a black Tanzanian oak inlay, British blue grasscloth wallcovering, and a beautiful painting like a Montague Dawson work are easy ways to achieve the effect. I think every room should have touches of black and gold in it; the colors appear throughout the design: in the picture frames, the fireplace grate, the floor, and even the architectural fragment lamps I picked up at a French flea market. Never be afraid to play with scale; large artwork, oversized furniture like the Louis Philippe desert server flanked by curvaceous chairs, and large accessories such as the antique knight sculpture fill a room but keep it clutter-free.
Photographs by Chris Davis

Above: The entryway had great bones: soft grey and white marble, a fine square shape, and the gilt French lantern. I took a very wide wallpaper border and cut various strips to trim out the room, outlining and defining the dado, millwork, casings, and doors, for a sense of cohesion. A hand-hooked rug that features classic elements—scroll work, sunburst patterns, bold borders—was inspired by the flooring and room's shape. The gold mirror frame and gold wall sconces, combined with black candles, lamp shades, and chair cushions, give the room a handsome, polished look.

Right: A very long, curved sofa is the perfect seating solution for a room with a large bay window. I love combining straight lines with curves. The elements appear in the square quality of the window panes, the couch cushions, and the antique rug. Antique French walnut side tables and a glass and iron tête de cheval coffee table bring sexy, fluid lines to the room.
Photographs by Chris Davis

"You don't need a lot of space to make a stunning room."
Cindy Galvin

Top: Red tones and other lively colors are perfect for dining rooms; they stimulate conversation and help promote a feeling of home. A late Napoleon period chandelier and Regency period gilt mirror over the buffet are stunning. I applied silverleaf paper to the ceiling to reflect even more light at night. A long oval rug in the rectangular room softens its linear features.

Bottom: An antique Gracie wallpaper screen was repurposed for the closet doors in a serene dressing area. Tall mirrors, soft upholstery, and a fine palette of muted greys showcase the stunning turquoise art. A wire chandelier from a flea market in France is feminine and delicate; it's the perfect crowning accessory for the retreat.

Facing Page: In light-filled rooms, you have more flexibility when playing with colors. Vibrant hues in accessories and accent tables, dark finishes on walls, and bold prints on furniture are ideal for such open, airy spaces.
Photographs by Chris Davis

Above: For an owner's weekend retreat, I used muted tones of beige and taupe in a range of textures and finishes to create a harmonious environment. Different textiles in this monochromatic palette make the space flow naturally from one area to another. The rustic light fixture made from wine barrel oak strips, the bulbous mercury glass vase, and the arched fireplace niche stand out against the square table and other linear elements in the room. Old bootmakers' forms used to create lamps for the equestrian homeowner and a limestone fireplace surround lend warmth to this modern day take on an Old Virginia farm.

Facing Page Top Left & Bottom: Only one wall was without windows, so I had to build off of that feature. The bar area, work space, and bookshelves run along the back wall, behind the large sectional sofa. Pops of blue throughout soften edges and lend a feminine feel to the very handsome design.

Facing Page Top Right: I kept it simple in the kitchen. L-shaped countertops, a huge island, and saddle-inspired barstools make the heart of the condo the perfect place for entertaining. The recessed panel cabinets with beadboard paneling and grey-washed island are tailored and welcoming.
Photographs by Kimberly Gavin

Bryan Bilczewski Design

Lauded by Chicago's Merchandise Mart Design Center and the city's Fashion Group International, designer Bryan Bilczewski blurs the boundaries between traditional and contemporary while relying on clean lines, rich textures, and premium materials to mediate his highly praised creations. As the principal of his own firm, Bryan consults with a trusted team of skilled builders and craftsmen to ensure custom-made outcomes of distinctive style. With a degree in interior design and a plurality of projects commissioned by Chicago's elite, his artistic stroke has stretched to Manhattan and Palm Beach with much recognition along the way.

Above Left: Frequent trips to the Windy City encouraged St. Louis-based homeowners to seek out a weekend retreat. The selected pied-à-terre, perched 55 floors above the Magnificent Mile, offers mesmerizing views of the lake and city, which precluded the need for window coverings. An original painting by emerging artist Willie Kohler adds vibrancy to the rich interior palette.

Above Right: Style, comfort, and forgiving fabric are not mutually exclusive with a guided eye. For homeowners who loved their large-breed dogs,, all three elements were non-negotiable. I had a 10-foot-long sofa constructed for space to sprawl, and covered it in Clarence House mohair fabric that's both decadent and tolerant. Sepia-toned photographs of Chicago's lakefront, Vaughan table lamps, and Mariette Himes Gomez cocktail tables add definition and elegance to the urban sanctuary.

Facing Page: The interior for a Chicago-based family's year-round retreat was inspired by the great outdoors. Located in the heart of Utah's Deer Valley, the home is surrounded by lush landscapes and an active culture. Hardwood floors were installed and the previously bleached ceiling was stained dark to add warmth. Accented by rustic yet refined furnishings, a neutral tone-on-tone technique echoes the natural beauty found outside. A custom hand-stitched leather table, ratcheted chair by Formations, and a pair of seven-foot-tall wall sconces by Ironwares International elevate the space from a typical mountain lodge. An original painting on a wood panel by artist Ed Ott further complements the natural aesthetic.
Photographs by Bryan Bilczewski

Above Left: Originally constructed with an exaggerated, 18-foot-tall vaulted ceiling, the bathroom was a major redesign from top to bottom. The ceiling and walls were tapered down to 12 feet and I installed cove lighting behind crown moulding for soft illumination. His-and-hers cabinets, from my own design, support the vanity while over-scaled mirrors with dramatic arches complement the design. Large Italian marble tiles offset by insets of Ann Sacks forged bronze tiles create pattern as a floating zinc tub by Waterworks piques interest in the corner.

Above Right: The corner of the master suite proved to be an ideal place to situate a large-scale chinoiserie secretaire. The dome-topped and lacquered piece is flanked by a Woodland chair in Lee Jofa fabric. Layers of drapery running wall-to-wall with Beacon Hill silk and Samuel & Sons trimming further the refinement.

Facing Page: The master bedroom of a French-style manor on Chicago's North Shore needed to be both relaxed and elegant. A 24-square-foot Tibetan flat-weave rug acts as a canvas for the cool-toned blue and gold room. To balance the copious amounts of fabric surrounding the windows, I designed a custom canopy covered in Beacon Hill silk to frame the bed and dressed it in embroidered fabric by Ebanista. Venetian plastered walls, perimeter crown moulding, and cove lighting add to the calm ambience in both the bedroom and bath, where a chandelier by Ironwares International hangs in opulence.
Photographs by Bryan Bilczewski

Connelly Interiors

James Connelly is an artist who has loved interior design since childhood. After working in the design industry for nearly 20 years, in 1996 James founded Connelly Interiors, a thoroughly full-service firm. Ready to design a home literally from the ground up, Connelly Interiors includes its own warehouse and delivery company, which gives James supervision of the entire process. Operating exclusively on referrals, James loves figuring out how to mold a homeowner's tastes into an extraordinary reality. Although primarily a traditional designer, James knows no bounds when it comes to making a space classically beautiful. He is constantly on the lookout for new ways to integrate tried-and-true design concepts into modern lifestyles that are reflective of homeowners' personalities.

Above: Inspired by the homeowners' extensive travels and their vision to blend the beauty of the Georgian era with a current, modern look, the loggia's black and white marble floor and the 18th-century urns harmonize beautifully to emulate a contemporary lifestyle.

Facing Page: The vibrant, hand-painted silk wallcovering sets a dramatic tone for the room, while the edgy Tony Doucette chandelier and geometric rug energize the space. Comfortable Regency armchairs surrounding a custom Oscar de la Renta table encourage relaxed conversations among family and guests.
Photographs by Eric Poggemann

Above: As an extension of the kitchen, the smartly tailored gathering room, with its understated elements, serves as the perfect backdrop for the homeowners' artwork. When the paintings change, so does the room's personality, underscoring the strength of the design. The geometric cobalt blue counterbalances the soft gold hues and adds to the feeling of warmth, welcoming friends and family members to read, visit, or relax.
Photograph by David Bader

Facing Page Top: A quiet palette of timeless design in the living room gives the space a fresh feel. Clarence House and Rogers & Goffigon fabrics balance the classic sisal carpet. An Amy Howard oversized cocktail table offsets the traditional furnishings. Simplicity of space guarantees that the patina will grow richer and more inviting over time.
Photograph by David Bader

Facing Page Bottom Left: The loggia intentionally includes minimal furnishings, insuring that the paintings and the view of the perfectly manicured courtyard capture the eye. The sleek silk labyrinthine fabric pattern echoes the sheen of the marble.
Photograph by Eric Poggemann

Facing Page Bottom Right: Whether chatting with friends or building LEGO creations with their youngest, the homeowners are able to enjoy the contemporary styling of the family room's luxuriously comfortable Donghia furniture with fabrics inspired by nature.
Photograph by Eric Poggemann

"A room's composition has many layers; no one piece should ever shout for attention."
James Connelly

"Style is everything."
James Connelly

Above: Patterns of clean, classic carrara marble reflect a sense of history and pure elegance in the master bathroom. The high-contrast silhouette wallcovering and the polished chrome fixtures add to the regal feel of the intensely personal space.

Facing Page Top: Traditional elements of marble, wood, stainless steel, and mirror give a gourmet's dream kitchen a youthful spirit. The combination of sapphire blue and bright white adds a fresh and contemporary yet familiar contrast to the Vaughn fixtures, hand-planed wood floors, and elegant cabinetry.

Facing Page Bottom: In the conservatory, clean lines and simplicity reign. The space is drenched with both natural luminosity and light from the McLean lantern, both of which are maximized by reflections in the lustrous marble and glass table. Minimalistic in design, the McGuire rattan chairs add a natural, inviting element. It's an airy, peaceful space with a quiet sense of well-being, a place to enjoy the beauty of the world.
Photographs by Eric Poggemann

Dazzling Designs

After working as a financial controller, corporate purchasing manager, and general manager in the automotive supply industry, Donna Brown of Dazzling Designs began following her second passion in 1991. Her training and experience in her first career influences her approach to interior design; project management with an accountant at the helm means spaces are completed in record time and with impressive efficiency—not many designers can finish a room torn down to the studs in a month. For Donna, thinking outside the box comes naturally. More often than not, she starts from the ground up: building a room around a beautiful rug that serves as artwork on the floor. Playing with scale, mixing textures, and always maintaining functionality, Donna follows a very specific project work plan for every space to create detailed rooms that make people want to take a second look.

Above: Focusing on the island—the Crema Boudeaux granite slab determined the size of the room—the kitchen boasts a variety of textures and finishes. Iron, wood, granite, and Venetian plaster keep it from being a stuffy, boring space. Three different wood finishes—sage green island cabinets, ivory wall cabinets, and cherry cabinets over the stove—lend a modern feel to the traditional design.

Facing Page: The Indian rug in the family room creates a solid foundation for the design; its reds and blues are mimicked throughout the room. The red chenille sofa and coordinating chair-and-a-half face the impressive fireplace. Fringe pillows, an iron chandelier, and leather ottoman with an oversized tray for serving make the room the perfect space for conversation and family time. The vaulted ceiling is accentuated by the angled, wall-mounted drapes that frame the window.
Photographs by Rosh Sellars

Above: When both homeowners are professionals, the challenges for space and convenience are doubled. The dual workspace is loaded with luxury and great textures. From the cherry cabinets that hide printers and office supplies to the Italian marble mantel on the pass-through fireplace, the room is functional and comfortable, which helps turn work time into together time.

Left: In a complete redesign of the dining room, I blended existing and new items with antiques. The circa-1900 buffet—which stretches along eight feet of one wall, adorned with a mirror and detailed buffet lamps—is joined by the homeowners' dining table and china cabinet. To the tortoise-finish Chippendale chairs around the table, I added an unexpected twist by covering the end chairs with two fabrics: velvet on the bench and inside back, and a patterned silk on the outside back. Ceiling moulding painted with metallics and LusterStone wall finish reflect the light from the chandelier.

Facing Page: I started the formal living room with the rug and kept the homeowners' herringbone settees. The updated fireplace with its limestone mosaic, new black painted cabinets, metallic wall color, and LusterStone wall finish bring the traditional room into the modern era. Textured velvet chairs with cane backs, silk and fringe pillows, and silk drapery panels and valances update the homeowners' pre-existing items and dress up the space. The blue that is spread throughout the space is a classic look for any room.
Photographs by Rosh Sellars

Interior Enhancement Group

With a rare combination of left and right-brain thinking, Kelly Guinaugh enjoys both the design and project management aspects of her business. As the founder of Interior Enhancement Group, Kelly and her design team work to compose life-enhancing environments. She credits a childhood rich in the arts for her innate talent and appreciation for interiors, while her business acumen was sharpened by a degree in business. Kelly and her team at IEG seamlessly create beautiful, functional interiors that clearly reflect their clientele. They keep a watchful eye on the timelines and budgets, instilling complete confidence that all aspects of the project are being managed.

Above: The traditional dining room table, a family heirloom, anchors the eclectic room. The homeowners challenged us to create a room that incorporated these pieces while reflecting their current personal style. A unique contemporary buffet from Artifacts was chosen to offset the traditional table. The juxtaposing styles introduce a touch of attitude, furthered by pops of crimson and gold that bring the room to life. The application of Donghia's mica wallpaper to the ceiling creates an interesting twinkle as it catches the accent lighting behind the crown moulding.

Facing Page: The functional and stylish great room accommodates the busy daily life of a young family who works, plays, and entertains. Anchored by a custom area rug designed by IEG, the room achieves a well-traveled motif by incorporating worry-free furnishings such as a reclaimed wood cocktail table that has only enhanced with time and durable textiles that can withstand years of the busy family's activities. The striking wood beams provide architectural interest and direct the eye toward the antlers, a treasured trophy.
Photographs by John Hanson

Kathleen Newhouse

Interior designer Kathleen Newhouse loves a challenge. For her, each new space she designs is a chance to represent the homeowners' distinct story through a beautiful collection of furnishings, art, accessories, and architecture. Constantly in touch with her surroundings, Kathleen adeptly discerns how each room fits the existence of its inhabitants and builds her designs around those clues. Finding inspiration in everything from world travel to local nature, Kathleen uses her keen sense of color and talent for spatial planning to assemble exactly the right elements to complete a room. Knowing which pieces should take the spotlight and which should play a smaller supporting role results in sophisticated, fresh rooms that are classic yet comfortable.

Above Left: The open, inviting, and elegant living room offers Old World charm with modern-day amenities—truly the best of both worlds. The fabrics and monotone colors in the room define the space, with black working as a dramatic grounding color.

Above Right & Facing Page: The trick in an addition is to make sure the new portions of the home flow seamlessly into the original rooms. The library demonstrates clean, classic lines in a Regency style, allowing the architecture of the home to stand out; a dramatic chandelier, wooden beams, and a very high cathedral ceiling add to the grandeur. Tiered swags and panels—iridescent dark grey and gold swirl print, accented with beaded trim—on the windows offset the oversized limestone fireplace. Truly an exquisite room, the library is upholstered in a mix of chenille, leather, velvet, and silk.
Photographs by Norman Sizemore

"Never skimp on your home; it is an extension of your own personality." *Kathleen Newhouse*

Above & Right: A billiard room full of intricate woodwork flows seamlessly into the adjacent four-seasons room, where the combination of windows and skylights furthers the open feeling and offers tremendous views.
Photographs by Norman Sizemore

Facing Page: A gourmet's dream kitchen is the hub of the home, helping the hosts to entertain effortlessly and making every guest feel welcome. A design meant to maintain the home's architectural integrity makes the renovated space feel like it was created years ago, but top-of-the-line amenities keep it firmly grounded in modern function.
Photographs by Norman Sizemore

Following Pages: The owners wanted a more modern edge with a distinct ambience for their master retreat. The metallic accents and crystals not only update the room but add an elegant touch of glamour, while clean lines and a monochromatic color scheme keep the classic style sophisticated and timeless. A multitude of patterns, when in the same color family, add texture and interest without feeling too busy.
Photograph by Mike Mantucca

LNM Interiors

A fanatic for function, Lisa Natale believes that design should intertwine purpose with comfort in order to create the ultimate space. With a background in psychology and interior design, the principal of LNM Interiors—an acronym for her motto "live, naturally, modern"—benefits from both resources when communicating with homeowners and interpreting their style. Known for creating sleek, sophisticated spaces, Lisa layers fabrics and textures in a room to enhance its dimension. Harnessing inspiration from fashion, she is acutely attentive to runway trends and enjoys translating them into edgy interiors.

Above: I love using textiles and prints to create depth in a room. A cut-velvet and raspberry checkered fabric set against mustard striped wallpaper invites the eye to linger a little longer. The wool rug with regal silk accents anchors the space and communicates a sense of formality, while soft textiles indicate ease and relaxation.

Facing Page: Framed within the tumbled travertine, the hand-crafted medallion inspired the kitchen's design. Antique ivory and sleek black granite are a twist on the traditional French design, which adds interest without stealing focus from the intricate backsplash.
Photographs by Gregg S. Seltzer

L.V.L. Enterprises

For Linda Axe, the suggestion to return to design after being a stay-at-home mom has been advice worth heeding. After attending Parsons School of Design and raising her children, Linda started a silk flower arranging company where she was commissioned to create arrangements for museums and corporate locations. After some deliberation though, she did indeed go back to interior design, specializing in traditional styles. Garnering inspiration from antiques and art museums, Linda is still nothing if not practical; she believes in investing in high-quality pieces that will stand the test of time while reinventing designs based on what is already in the room whenever possible. No project is too big or too small for Linda and L.V.L. Enterprises, who has created everything from spacious interiors to the very minute details—draperies, linens, or artwork—of a room.

Above Left: The day room features the homeowners' private collection of World War I recruiting posters as well as large-scale models of World War I fighter aircraft, which are suspended from the ceiling. A sense of patriotism permeates the room, from the American flag artwork to the blue-and-white checked chairs.

Above Right: Separate from the main cottage, the bunkhouse contains two bunkrooms with four beds each. Natural lighting filters through the skylights in the wood plank ceiling, making it a welcoming place for guests to rest and relax. Built-in storage saves space and draws the eye to the whimsical artwork on the walls and blue skies above.

Facing Page: Another of the homeowners' personal collections adorns the home's original living room, with some of the 63 whirligigs mounted on overhead beams. We used some of the furniture original to the cottage, and the rough, straw-embedded plaster walls add a touch of historic charm.
Photographs by Dean Van Dis

Above: For a rustic look with a touch of whimsy, we featured more of the homeowners' whirligigs alongside folk art, lamps made from discarded copper stills, and hanging chairs in the screened-in porch. Vertical striped shades may be raised and lowered to let the sun in.

Left: The dining room is crowned with a light fixture manufactured by the blacksmith shop originally located on the cottage's property. The fixture was hung by the dwelling's first owner, who turned the cottage into a girls' dormitory in the 1920s. More skylights let the natural light from the outdoors into the room. Built-in hutches provide storage, while the unmatched dining chairs keep the design casual and inviting.

Facing Page Top: Added in 2008, the new family room houses more of the homeowners' whirligigs and World War I posters. Sometimes personal collections require a designer to create a brand-new space to display them, which is what we did in the new addition. The room is adorned with more folk art, expansive windows, and a spoke wheel chandelier, creating a rustic atmosphere while letting the outdoors in.

Facing Page Bottom: An expansive island and stainless steel appliances invite guests to gather in the heart of the home while giving the chef a modern place to prepare meals. The homeowners' collection of cows was incorporated into the design with the aim of resembling a cozy country kitchen.
Photographs by Dean Van Dis

Mark Radcliff interior

Design icon Billy Baldwin once said that "a person with a real flair is a gambler at heart." This is true for Mark Radcliff, principal of Mark Radcliff interior in Chicago, who is known for overlooking the rules and composing layered interiors of interest. With a fine arts degree in drawing and painting, Mark often finds his work described as a detailed portrait or a fascinating collage. The rooms are at once warm and sophisticated, timeless and trendy, cozy and eclectic. Refusing to be defined by one style specifically, Mark accepts an array of assignments that further challenge his talent and refine his exceptional eye.

Above: A pristine paint application, simple draperies, and warm lighting are essential when creating an attractive interior. I chose effortless drapes constructed from fabulous fabric to soften the bright green walls, which brings the space to life and pops against the brick and chocolate hues found throughout the loft. The teal Dorothy Draper chest is a delicious addition to my collection of quintessential period pieces.

Facing Page: The treasured antique doors from Paris act as a neutral backdrop for layered textures and colors in the living area. Original dimensions inscribed in French are extraordinary to me and allow for an intimate connection from homeowner to craftsman.
Photographs by Leon Ikler

Pleats Interior Design

A window can be a portal into the heart of a home, but for George A. Pavick, windows were the starting point for his fully-inclusive design firm, Pleats Interior Design. Since establishing the firm in 1989, George has cultivated designs well beyond the gorgeous windows he created during his early years in the industry. From his 4,200-square-foot showroom in Lansing's Old Town neighborhood, George is able to take on projects that require anything from designing from the ground up to single-room remodels. His projects are historically accurate and faithful to original style characteristics. Additionally, being environmentally friendly is of great importance to him. Embracing classic designs, George and Pleats Interior Design create homes that will stand the test of time.

Above: The LEED Gold certified home—a rarity in residential construction—was designed and constructed by Stevens Associates Builders in partnership with the homeowners, while I headed up the interior design. The library, with its fabulous outdoor views through the arches and gorgeous brickwork on the walls, is a cozy space for the music-loving homeowners to play or relax. The antique hand-woven Turkish rug complements the beautiful hardwood floors beneath. Carefully researched reproduction lighting and a collection of antique hand-colored etchings stay true to the Federal-style home.

Facing Page: The front center hall boasts custom balustrades, impressive dentil moulding, a grand staircase, and historically accurate 18-by-18-inch black and white granite and marble checkerboard tiles. At the landing, an oil painting hangs on a soft yellow wall. Long crystals hang from the chandelier, a Federal reproduction.
Photographs by Beth Singer

Above: Looking out onto over 50 acres of lush grounds, the orangery certainly lives up to its historical purpose—it's perfect for gathering, dining, and housing citrus trees. As the usual space for family meals, the room has tall ceilings that allow natural light to saturate the space on one end, and on the other the fireplace provides the focal point for a cozy seating area. The broken pediment that surrounds the reproduction mirror was designed by the builder. Antique oriental rugs, absolute black granite, and quarter-sawn oak floors are gorgeous in the grand, open space.

Facing Page Top: I researched and hunted for the rugs to place in the parlor. Found across the U.S., some of the rugs are antique and others are reproductions. The draperies are all silk, and all the oil paintings in the room and throughout the house are originals. A camelback sofa is a must-have in any Federal design, and the Martha Washington striped chairs and early-1900s refurbished Steinway piano are absolutely striking.

Facing Page Bottom: It was very important to find authentic color combinations. The dining room is a reversal of the parlor's gold and blue pairing. Both colors are historically accurate to the style of the home, an important feature when dedicating a design to a specific period. Henkel Harris furniture—a favorite manufacturer of mine— provides ample dining space for the family and their guests, and another reproduction chandelier hangs overhead.
Photographs by Beth Singer

"Good design can last forever."
George A. Pavick

"I like the design of a room to
have a timeless feel."
George A. Pavick

Top: With a gorgeous view of the golf course and lake, the living
room is a welcoming space. Antiques adorn the built-in bookcases
and the rustic, custom-built mantel I designed specifically for the
space serves as a striking focal point. I wanted to create a very
relaxed, casual feel to the room since this is a second home for the
owners, but even vacation homes deserve custom touches, like the
area rug. The cocktail table—which sits under a beamed 11-foot
ceiling—was built specifically for the space and to show off the
area rug.

Middle: A glazed, pickle-green island topped with mahogany adds
even more usability to the large kitchen. To better accommodate the
homeowner, who loves to cook, the cooktop area was built shorter
than the standard height for countertops. A farmhouse sink fits
perfectly into the timeless room.

Bottom: A cypress ceiling with an 18-foot peak is the crowing
element for the family room. I selected furniture that is easy to live
with, a faux-crocodile cocktail table, and a tobacco glaze over the
green walls. The room looks onto the golf course, and the colors
help bring the outside in. It's a room constructed on the principle of
simple comfort.

Facing Page: Reclaimed pine floors pair beautifully with an alder
wood trestle table and dining chairs made in France. The sideboard
is a French reproduction, and I just love the Lowcountry feel of
the home.
Photographs by Rob Kaufman

Reddington Designs

Carol Salb, president and owner of Reddington Designs, opened her firm in 1986 and has always worked with the assumption that homeowners should feel their home is a reflection of themselves. To this end, Carol and her team set aside their own personal tastes to help create a unique, well-designed space that portrays each homeowner's individuality. As a consequence, a personal relationship develops between the homeowner and the designer that enhances the entire experience for everyone. The result is a multifaceted approach which embraces all styles and forms of design, gifting homeowners with a space that is uniquely their own.

Above Left: The master bathroom—which was short on storage space before our redesign—benefitted from a hand-carved, built-in armoire. It provides space for both clothing and linens behind the intricately carved designs and solid brass hardware sourced from Italy.

Above Right: Curvy, velvet seating and silk draperies bring Old World elegance to the sitting area just outside the master bathroom in a suburban Chicago home.

Facing Page: The curved vanities and granite countertops of the remodeled master bathroom convey the homeowners' preference for classical interiors and European excellence. We designed special roll-out medicine cabinets in the columns which flank each vanity. In this way the design remains focused on the warmth of the walnut woodworking, impressive crystal lighting fixtures, and custom marble mosaic flooring while maintaining modern functionality.
Photographs by Scott Shigley

Susan Fredman Design Group

Luxury is often defined in terms of sumptuous fabrics, rich colors, sophisticated ambience, or refined accessories. Susan Fredman, Barbara Theile, Aimee Nemeckay, and Terri Crittenden of Susan Fredman Design Group also believe that true luxury comes from people exploring their individual styles and co-creating environments that nurture in every way. Consistent throughout every home by Susan and her nationally recognized team of designers is a dedicated focus on comfort, proportion, and scale—the elements essential to creating a space that you never want to leave.

Above & Facing Page: Classical architecture with traditional quoining details and columns is juxtaposed with the rural landscape in the thoughtful design for a musician and a car collector. Views of the lakes, wildlife preserves, and rolling hills on the 287-acre Wisconsin estate were maximized and unique elements were interjected to illustrate the personality of the homeowners. The foyer introduces the feeling of the home with its formal, classical architecture infused with pops of whimsy. A hand-carved tree trunk table base paired with upholstered chairs in the dining room further highlights the combination of natural and softer materials.
Photographs by Nick Novelli, Novelli PhotoDesign

"The experience of the home should be based on emotions translated through architecture and interior design." *Susan Fredman*

Above: For an Illinois family of six, spaces with flexibility for both large and intimate gatherings were important. Through a thoughtful combination of reclaimed materials next to contemporary furnishings, textures, and vintage pieces—including beams created from old barn wood, handrails, 18th-century cupboard doors attached to the beam in front of the stairway, and metal screens to hide the TV above the fireplace—a blank canvas was transformed into a livable work of art.

Facing Page Top: Since the family does a lot of holiday entertaining, the dining room was one of the most important spaces. To add a personal touch, the table was custom made onsite from reclaimed redwood and features an inset border with vintage jewelry and cufflinks—some from the homeowners' families—all secured in clear resin.

Facing Page Bottom: Materials were carefully selected for seamless transitions from the kitchen to adjoining spaces. Reclaimed wood with vintage iron brackets marry the kitchen with the living room, and stone connects the additional eating areas and back door. The large variety of materials used, including marble, stone, reclaimed wood, limestone, and stainless steel, as well as full-height backsplashes and brushed-bronze hardware, add just the right amount of drama to the space. A sliding marble backsplash behind the stove provides additional storage.
Photographs by Nick Novelli, Novelli PhotoDesign

Tigerman McCurry Architects

The basic principles of design and architecture apply in the design of every private residence, but the way in which they are applied is as varied as the inhabitants of the home. No one understands and adheres to this concept as well as Stanley Tigerman, FAIA, and Margaret McCurry, FAIA, principals at internationally known Tigerman McCurry Architects. Their genius is evident in their approach to the uniqueness of each project, whether the dwelling incorporates modern elements, references tradition, or artfully combines the two. With a combined seven decades of experience and educational provenance that includes Yale, Harvard, and Vassar, Stanley and Margaret create refined, innovative spaces that embody the purpose and preferences of their clientele.

Above & Facing Page: A limestone-faced residence built in the late 1920s was dramatically renovated architecturally and seamlessly carried through the design of the interiors. The family room, located in what was originally a three-car attached garage, references the '30s with its Art Deco style, creating a dramatic yet welcoming ambience. A rear staircase to the family quarters above projected into the room, but the stepped soffit detail around the fireplace makes it read as a deliberate and dramatic part of the composition. We incorporated a custom framed mirror and fire screen.
Photographs by Steve Hall, Hedrich Blessing Photographers

"To interact, question, challenge, and collaborate is the essence of a true architect." *Margaret McCurry*

Above & Facing Page Top: Continuity throughout the home is enhanced by the repetition of gold leaf-trimmed silk paneling, which adds verticality to the elevations. In the living room, Biedermeier recamiers anchor the space and are enhanced by swagged window treatments and a number of French antiques, including Ruhlmann sconces. New French doors in the dining room replace the original windows.

Facing Page Bottom: Our interpretation often begins with an elegant orchestration of styles and periods. The master bedroom graciously embraces the swan bed and lyre end tables, reconstructed from an image of original Italian Biedermeier pieces, while the dressing room whispers at the Art Deco era through 1930s Leleu chairs and an exquisitely designed marble fireplace and screen. The bespoke rug embodies an Arts-and-Crafts spirit.
Photographs by Steve Hall, Hedrich Blessing Photographers

Morgante-Wilson Architects, page 128

Besch Design Concepts, page 76

Interior Enhancement Group, page 104

Gregga Jordan Smieszny, page 94

Anna Marks Interior Atelier

Anna Marks, senior interior architect of Anna Marks Interior Atelier, combines her love of classic architecture, clean surroundings, and natural light to create graceful, livable spaces. A signature Anna Marks project utilizes light as a design feature. She plays with shadows that change every hour, and integrates the reflective qualities of her chosen materials and elements. It's a technique that reinvents the concept of bringing the outdoors in—and offers the occasional pop of surprise.

Above Left: An open floorplan allows for free-flow circulation and conversation. The central living space merges seamlessly into the kitchen camaraderie, while the two-story windowscape frames spectacular ocean views beyond.

Above Right: Looking to create a Zen-like atmosphere among the trees just outside the window, the master bathroom was designed to feature two gently sloping sinks set in identical his-and-hers vanities. When turned on, water from the faucets runs from one end of the sink to the other, reminiscent of the flow of a river. Design solutions—such as a recessed television behind a mirror that's revealed with a click of a button, hidden medicine cabinets, and concealed electrical outlets—are easily accessible, yet hidden, in the tranquil space.

Facing Page: Culinary artists find the kitchen contemporary yet functional. Fully equipped, it includes two dishwashers, a six-burner cooktop, a downdraft vent that lowers out of sight when not in use, a European-style pull-out pantry, and small appliances concealed behind a rolling garage door cabinet. A trellised divider sections the space and creates sculptural interest. With windowed walls on both sides of the divider, natural light and shadow dance throughout the home no matter where the sun may be.
Photographs by Troy Campbell Photography

"There's a theatrical drama to sunlight; it's different every day."
Anna Marks

Above & Right: After losing their '60s-style structure to a hurricane, the homeowners had the chance to start over from the ground up. The secluded office space, complete with a custom-built desk overlooking the beach, was built adjacent to the master bedroom to give the owners a quiet place to get away from it all. Custom paneling and Asian-inspired floor-to-ceiling custom pocket doors in the bedroom provide a backdrop for the bed and extra storage behind. Soft whites in both rooms mimic sandy beaches and sun-bleached driftwood, while vibrant turquoise and teal on the bed are reminiscent of the ocean.

Facing Page Top: Softening the divide between indoors and out was the primary design concept behind the home's rebuild. The first-floor ceiling is swathed in high-gloss white paint to reflect its surroundings, thus mimicking the sun's glare off the ocean. The aquatic theme of the eco-friendly wallpaper adds a playful feel behind the mirror, which was hand-crafted from driftwood by a local artist. The custom-designed, seven-foot walnut credenza was built specifically to anchor the dining space.

Facing Page Bottom: In the porch room—which was originally planned as an open-air space—low-profile furnishings keep the focus on the two expansive window walls that jut out from the house like a private pier. The cotton rug and casual chairs create a warm, comfortable place for conversation and relaxing.
Photographs by Troy Campbell Photography

Artists Concepts

Designers Chris and Heather Robb, a mother-daughter team, view interior design like a work of art. Each room they take on is a blank canvas, one they fill with color, pattern, and texture to create a balanced design imbued with visual depth. By holding thorough consultations before each project begins, Artists Concepts is able to extract a homeowner's personal style and transform it into a fitting design. Their fresh ideas and attention to detail make any space, whether a reposeful bedroom or a lively living area, feel at once highly functional and luxuriously comfortable. In the eyes of the homeowner, it is nothing short of a masterpiece.

Above Left: The room is actually three highly functional spaces: kitchen, family dining area, and family room. To add interest, we provided detail in the architectural elements, such as the trestle's bright and airy square pattern. To blend the spaces visually, we repeated the colors of black, maple, and red throughout the design.

Above Right: An eye-catching Tibetan chest serves as an interesting focal point in the hallway. While we used bold pieces, such as the chest, throughout, we were able to maintain harmony in the space by delicately balancing patterns and colors. To finish off the look, we incorporated the homeowners' collection of family pictures to give the design a personal touch.

Facing Page: In order to achieve a transitional setting, we blended timeless antiques with modern furniture. The room is highlighted by the repetition of red and black and features simple, straight lines. By extracting and reusing color and shape, we united several different periods of furniture as well as the room's multifunctional spaces. In doing so, we achieved an overall design balance.
Photographs by Tony Soluri

Bardes Interiors

Inspired by classical art and architecture, Cindy Bardes Galvin of Bardes Interiors interprets homeowners' imaginations into unique design. Utilizing an inspiration piece as a starting point—whether it's a teak and shell picture frame, a bold red lamp, or a vintage print—Cindy builds around what homeowners want to feel when they enter the space. Travel and nature provide further creative inspiration, and Cindy's personal goal is to gift homeowners with design that is elegant, harmonious, and accessible. Recognizing the need for such a resource outside of the bustle of Chicago, Cindy opened MAZE Home Store in 2009, which also serves as office for Bardes Interiors, to share even more design beauty with homeowners.

Above & Facing Page: The dining room and formal living room share a space immediately inside the front door. Bold architectural prints and accessories, such as the silvery-gold and blue wallcovering, the Chinese Elmwood screen, the French chandelier, antique rug, and the architectural remnant lamp, warm up a large space and make it feel cozier. Combining materials, as in the red marble and iron dining table and the powder-coated tubular steel and walnut coffee table, gives a modern edge to a traditional design plan.
Photographs by Chris Davis

Above & Right: In a long and narrow space, I gave the homeowners a monochromatic foundation for their design. A sectional that cozies up to the seven-foot-long Chinese daybed—used as a coffee table—provides ample seating on a scale large enough to fill the room. The mix of pillows in pops of black and red suggests an Asian influence. That influence pairs well with the oversized vintage advertisement posters and chic mid-century wallpaper. Woven rawhide and bamboo barstools seated before the bamboo cabinetry and calacatta marble countertops, paired with the dark wood of the floor, are wonderful modern elements for the Chicago home.

Facing Page: The apartment was located in a building constructed with an elliptical curve, so the bedroom and master bath were both narrower on one end. I had to modify the design to suit both the long and narrow rooms. Playing with the height of the ceilings by adding top treatments on the windows and hanging gorgeous light fixtures in both rooms helps to draw the eye upward. A soft rug in soothing colors warms up the bedroom, and a bold feature wall of glass tile in the bathroom directs the eye toward the center of each room, minimizing the effect of the long spaces.
Photographs by Chris Davis

Besch Design Concepts

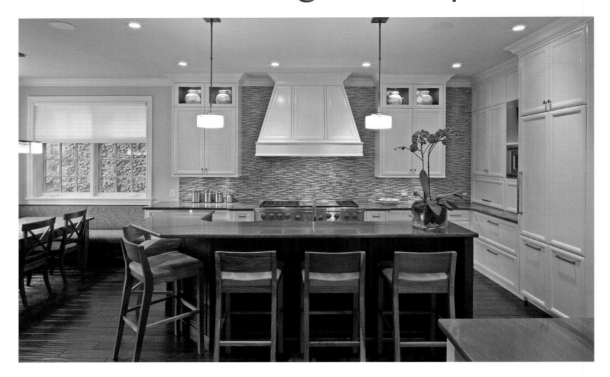

Architecture and design go hand in hand, so it makes sense that interior designer Susan Besch and her husband, architect Steve Besch, would eventually join forces. With over 20 years experience in the design industry, Susan decided to strike out on her own and founded Besch Design Concepts, where she draws on her own background in architecture to create cohesive, dynamic spaces for homeowners. Susan believes that proper space planning—the way you move in and out of a room, how it relates to other rooms—is essential to good design. Her mantras are to have an overall design plan and never compromise on quality, concepts that continually lead to engaging, exquisite designs.

Above: For a couple who loves to entertain, an open plan for the kitchen means that the home chef can easily interact with guests. Custom doors with pillow edges create an unusual depth to the cabinetry, and panels that glide along a hydraulic system hide small appliances from view. The hand-scraped hardwood floors and quartzite countertops are nearly indestructible—the perfect materials for a busy, energetic family. A glass mosaic tile backsplash and modern pendant lights contrast beautifully with the clean white cabinetry.
Photograph by Peter J. Nilson Photography

Facing Page: The master bathroom remodel took the room from an undersized, inconvenient space to a luxurious retreat. Following a cottage theme, specialized refinishers transformed basic hardwoods into faux exotics. Furniture skirting on the vanities keeps them from looking too much like cabinetry. Combined with the marble wainscoting and carrara marble floors with a green inlay accent, the bath has an exquisite Old World feel.
Photograph by Richard Lanenga Photography

Above & Left: We had a very large, nearly square room to work with and wanted to incorporate some dynamic details into the dining room. A double recessed trapezoid adorns the ceiling and a modern light fixture hangs from its center. Mixing old and new—the new furniture sits on a vintage rug—traditional and modern, the dining room becomes a vibrant space, perfect for entertaining. The butler's pantry, a segue between the kitchen and dining room, is functional and beautiful. Housing the homeowner's extensive collection of serving pieces, the space boasts pillow-edged cabinetry and quartzite countertops to match the kitchen.
Photographs by Peter J. Nilson Photography

Facing Page Top: Layering basic materials with high-end accents—an onyx countertop and backsplash, the copper glass bowl sink, and the detailed craftsmanship of the vanity with recessed pulls—makes the Zen-like bathroom something special.
Photograph by Richard Lanenga Photography

Facing Page Bottom: A Sub-Zero refrigerator, a washer and dryer pair—concealed within the cabinetry—and three ovens are just a few of the appliances we fit into the condo's kitchen. Bookmatched, horizontal-grain walnut veneer cabinets with custom hardware cut specifically for each door, paired with the 3.5-inch-thick quartzite countertop, give the homeowner the cooking space she craved.
Photograph by Richard Lanenga Photography

Previous Pages: For homeowners who entertain guests frequently, a living room that is cozy and intimate for family gatherings but ready for parties is a must-have. Hand-scraped wood floors extend from the adjacent kitchen, and parts of the homeowners' own art collection decorate the walls. Large leather ottomans serve as seating or serving spaces, and the pop-up television next to the grand fireplace allows the room to be used for football parties and elegant fêtes alike.
Photograph by Peter J. Nilson Photography

"The simpler the design, the more important the details become."
Susan Besch

Brian Clay Collins

In rooms designed to challenge and surprise, Brian Clay Collins sees his passions and the visions of his clientele come to life. Captivated by the decorative and fine arts, architecture, landscape design, antiques, and history, Brian found that interior design held the key to combining his interests into a career some would even describe as his calling. In his rooms, layers of texture and a mix of design styles make Brian's eye for detail apparent. Creating such combinations is a favorite design exercise for him; it reflects the reality of how most people acquire and collect special pieces throughout their lives. In this way, a room designed by Brian becomes autobiographical for the homeowner and leaves visitors craving more.

Above & Facing Page: In the Bi-Annual Detroit Junior League Show House, a home built in 1928 with a water view of Lake St. Clair, the library sitting room provides the homeowners with an intimate retreat. With a cozy sitting area in front of the fireplace, the room holds no electronics—I wanted it to be specifically for reading, conversation, and quiet contemplation. The walls are covered in reclaimed, antique paneling with a highly carved façade that's almost ecclesiastical in tone. Behind the bar setup, the cream-colored upholstered screen with nailhead trim allows for the remaining exposed paneling to have even more impact. Maritime influences are spread around the room: large tortoise shells and crystal objects with a marine theme adorn the walls and furnishings. An impressive cream-colored Hermès scarf breaks up the dark tones and provides a great conversation piece for visitors.
Photographs by Jeff Garland

Above: It's best to keep a delicate balance in guest bedrooms; you don't want it veering too masculine or too feminine lest it be uncomfortable for guests. In a circa-1926 Grosse Pointe Tudor Revival home, I used a pale aqua ceiling to set off the carved plaster moulding in tones of black, gold, and bronze metallic. The circa-1880 Danish secretary serves as a focal point and, except for this piece, I set the room arrangement on a bit of the diagonal to accommodate the tall column behind the bed. Additional 19th-century antiques are scattered around the room: a woven horsehair-upholstered Napoleon III chair is placed at a Biedermeier tea table that adjusts in height for multiple uses, while a Swedish zebra hide slipper chair sits below the window.

Right: A variety of textures keeps a room interesting. In the gentleman's bathroom of the Bi-Annual Detroit Junior League Showhouse, I used different textures along with a maritime theme to keep the eye moving. Alternating white and black commercial-grade vinyl wallcovering, hung horizontally, creates interest. The woven leather framed mirror, verde green marble, bleached linen shower curtain studded with French knots to resemble a sea urchin, wool rug, and tortoise-glazed porcelains keep the room from being a typical bathroom space.

Facing Page: Natural light became a decorative element in the home's second-floor sitting room; invigorating red in the morning light, it takes on an enveloping quality after nightfall. When working with a low ceiling, I like to draw the eye upward by hanging drapery right below the ceiling. I also added mirrored panels over the windows to extend the visual height and view to the outside. Framed Hermès scarves, a reproduction secretary with antiqued mirror doors, and splashes of animal print prove that a little bit of glamour is always welcome.
Photographs by Jeff Garland

Compass Design

Stacy Riley loves changing spaces, exercising her creativity, and bettering people's lives. After obtaining her bachelor's degree in interior design in 2001, two years later she founded Compass Design. A self-described transitional designer, Stacy loves to warm up a homeowner's vision of contemporary design or give a modern twist to something that otherwise proclaims traditional. She's always been interested in art and history, so upon entering a room Stacy immediately looks at its architecture— whether it's a bank of windows, sculptural fireplace, or vintage flooring—to guide the design. The belief that environments enhance a person's experience in a space, be it residential or commercial, drives her to create unique rooms for its users.

Above Left: High style was key to the design, but the fireside lounge—as we came to call it—had to be comfortable, and the fireplace wasn't even a part of the room to begin with. Limestone slabs flipped horizontally give the surround an updated feel while suiting the late-1920s home. Recessed areas for sconces lined with a warm, dark wood flank the fireplace. Custom chaise lounges fit the niches on each side, allowing for a place to relax.
Photograph by Anne Buskirk

Above Right: The original marble floors and beautiful floor-to-ceiling windows and doors at one end of the 1930s addition to the historic Booth Tarkington home built in 1911 had the tendency to leave the room feeling cold during winter months. Custom loveseats modeled after French 1940s sofa fashions, an inviting toffee color on the walls against black woodwork, and the rich camel of the window treatments warm it up. A soft, pebble-style rug and live plants soften the space and bring the outside in.
Photograph by Matt Thompson

Facing Page: The show-stopping master bathroon remodel features a custom curved vanity between the doorway and a curved tile wall that hides the shower. With a separate space for a seated vanity, the design boasts walnut veneer cabinetry, quartz countertops, and glass tile behind the sinks. Custom-made mirrors fit snugly onto the curved wall within frames of faux snakeskin. Art niches were created in the walls on each side of the vanity to house sculptural pieces of onyx.
Photograph by Matt Thompson

Darcy Bonner & Associates

Darcy Bonner, founder and principal designer of Darcy Bonner & Associates, LLC., knows how to turn a simple line into something sleek, graceful, and absolutely unforgettable. Whether he relies on the profile of a polished, modern dining table or the dramatic, fluid web of metal from a light fixture, Darcy uses the element of the line to enhance traditional classics and make his designs timeless. After earning dual master's degrees from Tulane University and the University of Illinois, Darcy founded Darcy Bonner & Associates in 1980, specializing in large-scale, luxurious projects where the classical and progressive intertwine to craft rooms unlike any other. With pops of vibrant color, juxtaposition of texture and materials, and always something a bit unexpected, Darcy's rooms are dynamic works of art.

Above: Clean lines of the dining table and chairs exemplify a classic motif with a modern twist. The table's finish reflects the statement piece of the room: a swirly, sculptural fixture suspended above the eating area. With dashes of orange against the tan, gold, and chocolate palette, the room encourages conversation and culinary delight.

Facing Page: Towering views and the soaring, spiral staircase command attention in the living space. Throughout the various sitting areas, traditional lines in the chairs and accent tables are striking against the chocolate paneling, stainless railing, and abundance of glass.
Photographs by Tom Rossiter

"Finding beauty in simplicity is the key to great design." *Darcy Bonner*

Above & Facing Page: Charcoal and graphite hues create a great backdrop for art collections, conversation-starting light fixtures, and bright bursts of color. Traditional furnishings and floral elements in turquoise, fuchsia, chartreuse, and royal blue are unexpected and draw the eye into the room.
Photographs by Tony Soluri

Fonda Interior Design

Rachael Franceschina, principal designer of Fonda Interior Design LLC, started designing in the mid-1990s in the urban design studio at Skidmore, Owings & Merrill in Chicago. Wanting to learn more about human interactions with interior environments, she soon found her place in the interiors studio serving worldwide corporate clients. Rachael earned her master's degree in interior design with an emphasis in human factors and ergonomics at Cornell University and is a professional member of ASID and registered interior designer in the state of Illinois. Her firm, Fonda Interior Design, LLC, is named in honor of her grandmother's business Fonda's Furniture & Interiors, which was in operation from the 1950s through the '70s. She credits her grandmother for inspiring her appreciation of the beauty of design, and Rachael has dedicated herself to intelligent and eco-friendly solutions. As a LEED accredited professional, Rachael loves to create healthy spaces and re-imagine existing pieces and fixtures.

Above Left: White subway tile, quartzite countertops, stainless steel appliances, and crown moulding update the kitchen remodel, which was a full tear-down and rebuild. Matching paint colors and hardwoods results in a seamless transition between the kitchen and attached family room. The farmhouse sink was a find by the homeowner, and we commissioned an Amish cabinetry company to build the custom cabinets.

Above Right: In the small dining room, I didn't want bright, strong colors to overwhelm the space but still wanted to create some colorful interest. Against the three-tone grey walls, the bright red Murano glass chandelier and Trina Turk for Schumacher peacock-print fabric absolutely pop. Although the table could accommodate six chairs, we chose to pair a bench with the vintage Dorothy Draper chairs rather than have two replicas produced. Black and white artwork about the room creates a large amount of visual interest without making too strong of an impact.

Facing Page: Once an un-insulated three-season room, the library was gutted to the studs. I installed cellulose insulation and an HVAC duct inside, while the exterior was clad in Hardie board, an eco-friendly cement board option. The mosaic limestone floor and the bold fabric on the windowseat cushion provided the design influence for the room. The Massive Paisley fabric by Maharam lends a playful, exotic feel.
Photographs by Betsy Maddox

Gregga Jordan Smieszny

Alex Jordan and Dan Smieszny are co-presidents and the creative minds behind interior architecture and design firm Gregga Jordan Smieszny. Founded more than three decades ago by the now-retired Bruce Gregga, the firm continues to create exceptionally edited, sophisticated interiors. As lead project director and designer, Alex credits his keen eye and affinity for fine art and antiques for making distinctive pairings, while Dan focuses on the architecture of each of the firm's projects— from small renovations to full-scale, ground-up designs. Examples of the firm's work have enriched the content of notable publications such as *House Beautiful* and *Architectural Digest*.

Above: The color palette applied to both the dining and living areas is anchored by the 1920s Swedish rug, signed MMF. A diverse collection of chairs adds sculptural interest to the living room. The homeowner's count a velvet-covered Art Deco lounge chair, based on a model from the French ocean liner SS *Normandie*, along with a Jean Michel Frank slipper chair and a reproduction Italian neoclassical armchair, to be among their favorite pieces.

Facing Page: In the newly built Lincoln Park townhouse, we incorporated French Moderne details, patterned terrazzo floors, and early to mid-century furnishings to create an energetic family home. The dining room boasts a spectacular 1950s Murano glass chandelier set above a lacquer-top Jansen dining table with a gunmetal and polished brass base. The pomegranate silk upholstered walls act as an ideal backdrop for the 20th-century Italian golfleafed sunburst mirror and sycamore and parchment sideboard inspired by an André Arbus design.
Photographs © 2010 Bruce Van Inwegen

Above: The study, adjoining the master bedroom, offers a place not only for work but also for relaxation. We chose two French leather chairs, circa 1930, and an Edward Wormley "sheaf of wheat" table to complement the French polished walnut paneling.

Facing Page: The master bedroom is dressed in cool, luxurious fabrics and evokes a sense of calm in an otherwise energetic home. The entrance to the room is highlighted by an intricate Venetian mirror from the late 19th century and introduces a majestic sleigh bed inspired by the work of Paul Dupré-Lafon. Inside the spa-like bathroom, a 1960s Swedish Orrefors glass fixture maintains the elegant style found throughout the rest of the home.
Photographs © 2010 Bruce Van Inwegen

HM Design

Heather Milligan wants to make the world pretty—or at least her little part of it. Intrigued by fashion from an early age, Heather envisions every room as if it were dressed in haute couture, but practicality also plays a role in her designs. She knows what's important: family, friends, and living life to its fullest. This perspective strongly influences her designs, a majority of which are completed for families with young children. As a designer who believes that homes should be livable—a place that provides relief rather than creates anxiety—her philosophy simply makes sense for the modern family. For Heather, great design isn't always synonymous with expensive or fragile; it has to first and foremost respect the homeowners' lives. By breaking the rules of scale and the preconceived notions of what is elegant, Heather creates rooms that are on par with the latest luxury trends but are ready for a family to enjoy together.

Above: Bold color makes a room; even a windowless basement can be a great place to gather if the colors and décor make you want to be there. A tremendous amount of time went into sourcing objects that are family-friendly because people have to live in the space. The Ralph Lauren coffee table is gorgeous and exceptionally well made—it stands up to daily use by children—and re-covered shabby chic sofas get a new lease on life in the playroom.

Facing Page: Eight-foot ceilings always pose a challenge. To make the most of them, the millwork on the mantel extends all the way to the ceiling to add height. Nero Marqina marble adds weight and glamour to the hearth; the mantel is dressy but whimsical, flanked by ceramic whippets below, and the Hahn Dynasty replica soldier collection atop adds another layer of detail. The lantern is an oversized but necessary addition, casting light on the rich red velvet and linen sofas—a HM Design signature upholstery practice. Sofas are unfinished without whimsically patterned pillows.
Photographs by Rick Drew

Above: A luxurious remodel, the home's former office was transformed into a fabulous closet with wall-to-wall sisal and mirrored doors. Gathered on the ottoman, magnums of Veuve Clicquot champagne adorned in limited-edition bright orange neoprene covers indicate that getting ready to go out can be as fun as the festivities to come.

Facing Page Top: In the luxurious master bedroom, the bed is draped with custom linens and accessorized with a black and silver sequin peace sign pillow. A collection of antique Swedish hand-colored architectural prints line the wall above the oversized headboard. Fun contrasts like the ornate chandelier paired with the burlap-covered wing chair give the room character and balance.

Facing Page Bottom: A demilune desk found at resale is dressed up by an upholstered chair and orchids. Jute rugs and an assortment of artwork with pieces hung below eye level lend a casual feel to the space.

Previous Pages: While the homeowner loves her entire home, the living room is the space that makes her the happiest. It is large enough to display all the collections she has spent time lovingly assembling. Antique portraits, a mixture of white plaster and black lava intaglio seals, architectural prints, and, most prominently, the 1920s replica of an ancient Greek bas-relief all blend seamlessly and best illustrate the owner's interests and passions. The Venetian velvet-upholstered Amy Howard daybed allows guests to sit back and peruse all the design books gathered on every surface. The background black and white paint—though dramatic in theory—grants a soothing finish to the space, adding depth and dimension.
Photographs by Rick Drew

"Loving where you live should be a mantra everyone lives by—it is not necessarily a luxury."
Heather Milligan

Interior Enhancement Group

Approaching each custom interior, from residential to commercial spaces, with the intent to "listen, inspire, and create," Kelly Guinaugh considers design aesthetics, lifestyle, and needs when interpreting her homeowner's desires. In order to achieve an authentic reflection of those wishes, Kelly stresses a culture of listening at Interior Enhancement Group, which has proven to be an award-winning trait since the firm's founding in 1999. It is notably the only interior design firm in the Chicago area to have achieved the Chicago Design Team top 10 designer award for seven consecutive years. The firm was also awarded best in design by the International Furnishings and Design Association for Illinois.

Above: A family transitioning from city living to a suburban setting appreciated clean lines that would balance with the traditional architecture of their new home. The dining room table, initially admired by the homeowner in a magazine photo, became their inspiration for the room. The table is a "wow" piece in the room and the square design is excellent for conversation with dinner guests. The ambience in the room is further enhanced by the pearlized, multi layered paints applied onto the ceiling; the walls are a metallic tissue blend that add just enough texture to make an elegant statement. Pleated silk from Kravet Fabrics was used for the window treatments, which offered another opportunity to bring additional texture, ultimately reflecting the homeowners' unique style.

Facing Page: The master bedroom's serene and timeless feel was achieved several ways. We upholstered the headboard from Kravet Furniture in a lush mohair fabric and then dressed the bed in silks, velvets, and chenille for an irresistible palette of alluring textures. Mirrors designed by IEG, an Artifacts nightstand in a beautiful painted patina, and crystal lamps add a touch of glamour to the luxurious bedroom retreat.
Photographs by John Hanson

Jenna Wedemeyer Design

As a designer, mother, and wife, Jenna Wedemeyer seeks calm in the chaos of everyday life. Likewise, many of her clientele require their homes to be accommodating to five-year-olds while aesthetically pleasing to adults. Jenna's priority as principal of Jenna Wedemeyer Design is to decipher her homeowners' particular style then elevate it. Working through communication and trust to understand how the families live, Jenna hears their histories and views their life's acquisitions. Her challenge is to bring it all together in a cohesive, unique way that reflects them and not her, becoming a curator and editor of their homes and possessions.

Above Left: I hung the clock face, salvaged from a French cathedral, on top of a stone mantel with a few, carefully edited pieces. The walls, painted in Benjamin Moore Navajo White, create an ideal canvas for the dark, contrasting furniture and objects.

Above Right: A restored antique English partners' desk—found at a flea market—displays a bronze from a husband to his wife after the birth of their second child. Old books and a pair of marble lamps provide substance and create an unusual collage of objects that rest next to an over-scaled wingback chair that I discovered in an alley and recovered in menswear wool.

Facing Page: A setting for family meals and fancy dinner parties has to be both multifunctional and tough. Delicate Travers linen backs the chairs that are otherwise covered with luxurious yet sturdy polyester velvet. The patina on the Niermann Weeks chandelier and antique dining chairs add age and depth to a brand-new home, while the organic sculpture offers a touch of whimsy to an otherwise organized space.
Photographs by Susan Kezon

Above: Pairing opposites creates tension in a space: small versus over-scaled, light versus dark, and old versus new. A George Smith Knole-style sofa upholstered in cowhide sits opposite bobbin chairs by Formations. An antique painted dresser found on a trip to Antwerp, as well as Italian hand-forged fireplace tools—given as a gift after the couple's wedding in Florence—complete the personalization.

Left: Floor-to-ceiling organic-shaped mosaic tiles from Ann Sacks juxtapose the linear nature of the mirror and vanity in a bathroom. The alabaster shades on the nickel wall sconces cast lovely shadows.

Facing Page Top: A peaceful bedroom acts as a sanctuary, especially when free from distractions and technology. The linen-draped bed is meant to mimic a cocoon adorned with pillows made of remnants of 19th-century Hungarian needlework. An angelic painting by Elizabeth Schnabel completes the intimate space.

Facing Page Bottom: We took particular care in the renovation of a 1920s Mediterranean-style home to preserve original features such as archways and stained leaded glass casement windows. The black and brass La Cornue range was custom-built in France; its chrome strapping highlights the pewter hood and island top made by a local artisan. Solid walnut cabinetry, crafted by builder Nunzio Fricano, is embellished with hand-cast bronze hardware from Lithuania; the end results are authentic and timeless.
Photographs by Susan Kezon

Jessica Lagrange Interiors

What began as a budding passion in college became a blooming career for Jessica Lagrange. As an intern at an architecture firm working in the color materials library, the now principal of Jessica Lagrange Interiors nurtured her strong interest in interiors and developed her artistic eye into a keen sense of design. While conducting a team of industry experts, she runs a personable residential design firm and refers to clientele as friends and family. Absent of a signature style, she and her team strive to stay fluid in order to meet homeowners' ever-changing needs and exceed their ever-expanding expectations.

Above & Facing Page: Displaying fine art—such as the Bertoia sculpture in the hallway—is essential to a homeowner who delights in collecting. Relocating from a suburban estate to an apartment in the city posed a predicament for a passionate wine collector and avid entertainer. We installed a hallway of temperature-controlled refrigerators lined with goldleafed mosaic tiles and back-lighting in order to showcase the homeowner's personal collection of fine art: wine.
Photographs by Tony Soluri

Above & Right: A solid foundation just looks richer. In a newly
constructed building offering 8,000 staggering square feet of blank
space, we applied hand-laid floors, brass olive knuckle hinges, and
intricate lighting to build up the current pied-à-terre. Interior
architecture sends a strong message of quality and truly makes
the home.
Photographs by Tony Soluri

Facing Page: In order to achieve an aged appearance, I applied layers of
paint to the newly built and paneled walls in classic tones of grey and
beige. Distressed wooden floors and walnut-framed furniture enhance
the home's sophisticated nature while rich fabrics imbue a sense of
calm and comfort.
Photograph by Nathan Kirkman

K Norwood Interiors

After personally restoring two historic homes, Karen Norwood realized that her new passion required more than time and enthusiasm; it demanded a discipline. Inspired by the work of design maven Billy Baldwin and others, she returned to college to obtain a degree in interior design—with a certification in European art, architecture, and furniture design—as a prelude to embarking upon a new career. Since that time, Karen has been a peer group leader and committee member for Chicago's ASID designers, where her local involvement has garnered her influence and a number of industry awards. Often motivated by the works of other leading designers such as Juan Pablo Molyneux and Darryl Carter, along with books such as *Dwellings* by Stephen Sills and James Huniford, she approaches each project mindful of the homeowner's taste and style—allowing beauty, simplicity, and comfort to be the driving force behind a project's evolution.

Above: We assembled the new kitchen materials around colors found in the granite counters preserved from the home's first renovation. In order to accommodate a taller style cabinetry, we raised the ceiling and selected Mission-style doors with a weathered slate—which required a three-process, hand-painted finish—for a clean and modern look. Seeded glass was added to several of the doors for a touch of elegance, while multitoned glass tiles in plum, opal, charcoal, and taupe were chosen for the backsplash as a unifying collage of all the elements.

Facing Page: Guests are greeted by a collection of black and white images by Willy Ronis depicting life in post-war Paris and Provence along with an iconic photograph by Lillian Bassman. A Rill table by Bill Sofield for Baker is dramatic in scale, having a gold rice inset top and ebony lacquer base. A Sakki Taylor mirror hung against Phillip Jeffries tuxedo wallpaper adds to the glamorous ensemble.
Photographs by Susan Kezon

Above & Facing Page Top: A combination living and dining room requires both entertaining and dining areas. The living room furniture is arranged in a 'U' configuration to maximize flow and conversation, while a round dining room table for four expands into an oval table that can accommodate eight. The scale of the furnishings and fabric selections—a calming palette of champagne, earthy browns, and seafoam blue—was chosen to complement the view of the cityscape and expansive lake beyond the east-facing windows. Traversing sheers by Bergamo lined with satin fringe add architecture and height to the wall of windows. A delicate bracelet lantern with linked glass tiles made by designer Thomas Pheasant hangs over the Lucien Rollin zebrawood table. Above is a commissioned painting by Chicago artist Francine Turk that, when examined closely, incorporates the words from the couple's wedding song.

Right & Facing Page Bottom: The great room, used for entertaining, dining, and relaxing, received a striking yet understated palette of violet, smoky taupe, ebony, and tobacco wood. The walls and vaulted ceilings are washed in a silver-satin finish and a custom rug, co-designed and produced by Hokanson, anchors the sitting area with silk stripes of lilac, violet, and white on taupe wool. The fireplace was resurfaced in a smoky taupe Athens Grey marble by Ann Sacks, which plays off the linear patterned area rug. A custom bronze spiral chandelier by R. Jesse echoes the spiral staircase ascending from the loft to the rooftop garden, complementing the owner's favored treasure: a refurbished 1920s German Knabe piano. Personal art above the fireplace and throughout the home provides sentimental memories of places visited during the homeowner's lifetime of travels.
Photographs by Susan Kezon

Kai Behnke Interiors

With a background in fashion merchandising and a passion for interior design, Kai Behnke of Kai Behnke Interiors decided to make a dramatic career change after 25 years as a flight attendant. Following design school and her work for Pierre Deux, Kai set out to craft beautiful, soothing spaces for creative and artistic homeowners. Drawing inspiration from her travels and the world around her, Kai describes her style as classic with a personalized twist. Whether juxtaposing unusual color schemes with natural elements or monochromatic palettes with metals and manmade textiles, Kai works to create a place of balance, harmony, and comfort where homeowners feel recharged by the space they call home.

Above: Rich custom bookcases are crowned by a coffered ceiling in a luxurious library that's adjacent to the foyer. The grand, open floorplan is divided between the rooms by limestone columns. I love mixing elements like leather, metal, and architectural details to create a visually interesting space that remains comfortable.

Facing Page: A hair-on-hide chair with a custom antler table is a bold element in an informal family room. In an effort to provide an extra sitting area in the family room, I designed a space that emulates the homeowners' love of the West and provides a view of the magnificent outdoor garden and multilevel desks from which the Chicago skyline can be enjoyed.
Photographs by Michael Klug

"Home should be a place of inspiration, nurturing, and comfort." *Kai Behnke*

Above & Facing Page Bottom: In a Chicago penthouse overlooking Lake Michigan and Millennium Park, I used nature as the inspiration in the open floorplan to make the room feel like an extension of the outdoors. The Venetian plaster in matte chocolate brown was specifically matched to the custom-designed area rugs, made of wool and silk, which gives it a subtle texture. Used on the fireplace surround and the foyer walls, the plaster is carried through the entire penthouse. The room's focal point is the breathtaking view out the full wall of windows, and when entering the penthouse, Tom Corbin's *Woman with Bird* sculpture emphasizes the beauty of the skyline behind it.

Right: Inspired by the homeowners' unique art collection, I updated existing furniture pieces with bold pops of persimmon and blue that look vibrant against the animal-print carpeting, dark moss-colored walls, and neutral chairs. The Asian buffet adds color, storage, and lighting while providing a showcase for one of the owners' favorite works for art.

Facing Page Top: A hammered metal loveseat upholstered in rich brown leather provides a wonderful foundation for the painting above. Enhancing the work, the loveseat allows the painting to be the focal point while still remaining an interesting and luxurious part of the master bedroom sitting area.
Photographs by Michael Klug

Lara Prince Designs

A home should be a fun, comfortable haven for all family members, reflecting their unique character and lifestyle. That is what designer Lara Prince achieves; her spaces foster creativity and expression while standing up to the everyday lifestyles of active homeowners. Inspired by her lifelong passion for good design, Lara left her career in the financial world for fashion before she decided to pursue her degree in interior design. In 1999, Lara struck out on her own and founded Lara Prince Designs, Inc., a firm that's all about originality and style. Initially hailing from Manhattan, Lara creates works that are edgy, inspired by rock and roll, and utterly luxurious while still making sense for the modern homeowner. She knows what it means for pieces to be family friendly, and she artfully combines durable designs with high-end elements to transform a space from ordinary to downtown chic.

Above & Facing Page: When I got my hands on the house, it was so "vanilla." There was no depth, texture, or character, but I loved its great architectural features. Beautiful angles, archways, mouldings, and coffered ceilings were some of the existing bones I was excited to work with. Thinking outside the box by combining sexy wallpaper, unusual found objects, and mid-century furnishings gives a room a soul. Thoughtful design is not an arrangement of coordinating furniture, fixtures, and textiles, but rather a vignette of hand-picked pieces that have an integrity to stand out on their own yet somehow come together to create an atmosphere that livens the senses and emotions.
Photographs by Tony Soluri

Above: I fell in love with the wallpaper years before it dressed up the dining room; it really gives a funky contemporary twist to a very traditional setting. The dining table is a work of art in itself; charred throughout, the surface is then distressed with a chainsaw and treated so that it's nearly indestructible. I hung a chandelier made of strips of bone and crowned with a horsehair shade over the table. High-end pieces like the fixture and table can be easily paired with ready-made elements. The reproduction chairs look just as luxurious as the table they surround.

Right: An antique English sideboard—goldleafed and adorned with graffit-style lyrics from John Lennon's "Imagine" and "Give Peace a Chance"—draws guests inside as soon as they step into the entryway. I love the juxtaposition of the piece with the mid-century chandelier above. They are from entirely different eras and stylistically worlds apart, but they work beautifully together. Quite often wallpaper makes a big enough impact that art becomes less urgent to adorn a space. Sometimes an interesting and dynamic piece like the sculptural mirror above the sideboard is a nice alternative to a painting.

Facing Page: Rugs do so much for a room; they can bring a scheme together and warm up a hardwood floor. Purple tones—sometimes more plum, other times with a blue undertone—are evident throughout the home. Mid-century décor, from shelf solutions to art and light fixtures, makes for a playful tone and is combined with natural elements to create a warm and casual tone.
Photographs by Tony Soluri

Lisa Smith Interiors

For Lisa Smith, designing a room is like working through a puzzle. From the founding of Lisa Smith Interiors in 2002, she has embraced her lifelong passion for interior design and brings elements of a room together to create an exceptional work of art—much like completing a puzzle. Design thrills Lisa, who approaches each project with the enthusiasm to create rooms that are both elegant and approachable. For her, designing a room means never compromising on quality; luxurious textures, authentic materials, and fine finishes add timeless appeal that lasts. Her taste is exquisite, her attention to detail is impeccable, and the result is sophistication and comfort in design.

Above Left: The study off the master suite is a serene space, with grasscloth wallpaper providing a supporting backdrop for an exceptional feathered walnut chest. The antique gold mirror hangs opposite a favorite painting, reflecting the custom piece, which was a gift from a favorite homeowner.

Above Right: The herringbone pattern on the floor and the stately mouldings define the gallery hall as more than a segue between the master suite and kitchen. Boasting views of the meadow on the back side of the property, the hall is a destination of its own. The contrast between the white mouldings and dark chocolate mahogany doors creates a bold yet elegant surrounding. At the end of the hall stands an antique dish cabinet, which welcomes people into the kitchen.

Facing Page: A true great room in both function and design, the foyer transitions seamlessly into the living room and then dining room to create the ultimate gathering space. The soaring ceilings defined by wood beams add architectural significance. At the far end of the room, raw silk draperies with banded silk trim frame the dramatic window and the Winterthur-inspired linen sofa. The classic marble urn is a favorite piece and the silver collectibles are family heirlooms—accessories should reflect something about the people living in the home.
Photographs by Kendal Reeves

Morgante-Wilson Architects

Principals Elissa Morgante and Frederick Wilson, collaboraters since 1994, when Elissa joined Frederick's 1987-founded firm, work together to design homes literally from the ground up. With expertise in architecture and interiors, a respect for traditional and modern design, and a sensitivity to the environment in which a home is located—whether in a historic district or on a beach—the team at Morgante-Wilson Architects produces timeless and original homes. While Frederick excels at looking at the big picture, Elissa flourishes while designing the subtle details of a space. Teaming up with their homeowners, Elissa and Frederick create residences that challenge convention and always make an impression.

Above & Facing Page: Four contemporary club chairs with a metallic floral design define the seating area of the open concept living spaces. The dynamic light fixture, suspended from the second floor through the home's center, hangs over the round table of the dining room. Curves in the home's architecture are mirrored in the lines of the light fixture and the room's furnishings.
Photographs by Michael Robinson

"Good design extends beyond drawings and floorplans. Good design evokes emotion and a sense of well-being." *Elissa Morgante*

Above: The sunroom acts as the ultimate seamless segue between the interior of the home and the stunning views of Lake Michigan. By combining traditional and modern elements, such as the coffered ceiling and the rug with an organic vine pattern laid along geometric lines, the space is elegant and comfortable. Cane chairs face the lake through French casement windows; the view is easily seen over the low-profile contemporary sofa. Sheer draperies soften the lines of the windows without obscuring the view. Based in tradition, the design of the home creates a stunning experience; its interactions with the environment are different as you travel from room to room.

Right: A wall of windows gives bathers in the freestanding soaking tub sweeping views of the lake to enjoy while relaxing in the elegantly peaceful bathroom suite—with or without lake breezes.

Facing Page: We built the home with the lake views in mind; the structure curves in an arch to capitalize on the vistas. Each vantage point is unique, and the shore is seen from every room in the house. The muted color palette and an emphasis on natural materials throughout reflect the elements just beyond the home's windows. They work together to create a space that is cohesive and in sync with the surrounding environment.
Photographs by Michael Robinson

Paul Lauren Design Consultants

Lauren Rautbord of Paul Lauren Design Consultants finds inspiration in the world around her, but especially from her travels. Influenced by the European ideal of keeping life simple in the most beautiful settings, Lauren's high-end designs begin with a neutral color palette. To this she adds color when necessary and texture, which she is willing to spend good money on; cashmere, velvet, mohair, linen, and silk are all well worth the expense. Lauren believes that a room should always feel good. A pretty design garners compliments, but a comfortably welcoming room is one that people will want to return to again and again.

Above Left: A relatively monochromatic color palette draws attention to the room's details: the matte finish chandelier, the patterns on the paneled wall, and the place settings.

Above Right: Far more interesting than cream or beige, green walls create a soothing environment in which owners can easily relax. Transparent draperies soften the light while still allowing it to filter into the room.

Facing Page: Mixing contemporary wall sconces with ornate, traditional entry tables adorned with modern accessories really expresses a transitional design. The patterned carpet and flush-mount mirrors on the wall are interesting and anything but stuffy.
Photographs by Jess Smith, PHOTOSMITH

Reddington Designs

Each design created by Carol Salb and her team at Reddington Designs is as individual as the homeowner. The psychological aspect of the design process is what thrills Carol the most; interpreting the fantasies of homeowners and delivering them in a way that reflects precisely who they are. To accomplish this, she relies on active listening, meaningful interaction, and strong intuition. Carol wants family and friends to be struck by the home's uncanny similarities to the homeowners' personalities. The balance of masculine and feminine energy, traditional and modern design aspects, and effective use of color and light are employed to successfully create these personal spaces.

Above: There are ways to transform an expansive great room into a cozy and inviting environment. We painted the ceiling the same deep shade as the grasscloth walls, installed a 60-inch mica chandelier, used wide-plank, dyed oak floors, and added velvet draperies for sumptuous texture.

Facing Page: We wanted to create a comfortable place for conversation with the addition of the hearth room. The combination of elements such as stone on the fireplace wall, cedar on the ceiling, woven wood shades layered with floor-to-ceiling draperies, oversized leather chairs, and a cast-bronze coffee table come together to create a warm, intimate feeling.
Photographs by Scott Shigley

"The most important variable in the design is the homeowners themselves. What is their lifestyle like? Who cooks? Who cleans? What are their hobbies? Where do their children drop their stuff when they come home? Where do they wash their dogs?" *Carol Salb*

Above Left: The entryway greets visitors with a mixture of textures and materials, from the deep wall color to the mother of pearl tile ceiling. At the top of the split staircase, art niches provide a nontraditional gallery for the homeowners' personal collection.

Above Right: A herringbone pattern of glass and marble creates the backsplash for the butler's pantry, which provides service to the dining room off the kitchen. We chose a darker stain for the walnut cabinets to differentiate the space while keeping it cohesive with the kitchen's décor.

Facing Page Top: The kitchen, formerly the home's great room, features a see-through fireplace flanked by built-in wine refrigerators. The creation of the 14-foot granite-topped island required consultation with a structural engineer to provide an extra-deep dining counter with as little visible support as possible. With the remodel, the kitchen truly became the heart of the home and the favored place for the homeowners and their guests.

Facing Page Bottom: It's always a challenge to subtly incorporate a 60-inch TV screen into a beautiful room. The custom-designed cabinet, constructed of sapele wood with carbalho wood accents, is so stunning that the TV becomes a complement, rather than a detriment, to the space. The cast-bronze pulls were the inspiration for the crown detail. The easy flow into the kitchen, hearth room, and formal sitting room with built-in bar make the home perfect for entertaining.
Photographs by Scott Shigley

RS Design Studio

The serendipitous intersection of two disparate things innately yields a beautiful result. Randy Shingledecker of RS Design Studio has eloquently merged the worlds of architecture and interior design, as well as the genres of traditional and contemporary, to form a uniquely cohesive approach to his creative work. Focused on developing whole environments rather than simply a collection of pieces and parts, the architect-cum-designer utilizes an artist's palette of light, scale, texture, and years of experience and ingenuity for projects of all scopes. His transitional designs nod to the past but are clearly focused on the future, which creates an intriguing look sure to stand the test of time.

Above: Working with an unusually gracious open area, I designed the 65th-floor condo in River North to have a variety of seating areas that make sense individually as well as collectively. The residents' cherished artwork—composed by a Japanese artist using handmade papers and natural dyes—serves as the focal point of the main living area and as inspiration for the whole home's color palette.
Photograph by Mike Crews

Facing Page: Because I was able to collaborate with the architect from the earliest design stages, the Lincoln Park home's interior has a very architectural look and feel. Elements like the dramatic fireplace wall—made of a single piece of wood—bookshelves, and wall of windows lend themselves nicely to a carefully edited collection of furnishings and flourishes. The horsehair rug from Argentina is wholly unexpected and adds wonderful natural character and texture. Overall the space is grounded with traditional pieces but curated to have a warm, modern vibe.
Photograph by Agnes Donnadieu

Ruth Casper Design Studio

Inspired by the philosophy that home is a sanctuary, Ruth Casper founded her firm, Ruth Casper Design Studio, LLC, in 1997. With an eye toward helping homeowners realize their design visions, Ruth emulates the unique style of those who live within a home's walls. Specializing in floorplan design, space planning, and project management, Ruth guides homeowners through their new home or remodel design from start to finish, including lighting and fixtures, color palette coordination, flooring, and custom textiles. Compelled to make bold choices, Ruth creates designs that are characterized by their dynamic movement, use of color, dramatic touches, and the cohesive combination of design styles.

Above: The goal of the family room was to mix textures soft to the touch to create a comfortable, relaxed, elegant style. Using a variety of materials for tables—a custom-designed double-layered iron coffee table, a petrified wood end table with polished chrome legs, a honey-washed console table, and a metal lattice end table—not one is the same, but each complements the other. Recessed lighting and a neutral wall color showcase bold artwork. Textile patterns are repeated throughout the room in the pillows and footstool, and match the large sculptural pieces behind the cozy sectional.

Facing Page: An intimate breakfast nook is the perfect place to read a book or host a game night with friends. The custom stained, distressed, and glazed table and chairs cozy up to the stone fireplace. Adorned with chrome candlesticks and crowned with a luminous modern fixture above, the table setting embraces nature with a touch of glamour.
Photographs by Paul Konkal Photography

Above & Right: Bold color and balance of pattern create a
sophisticated space, inviting family members to pull up a custom-
designed floor cushion or lounge and watch movies. No matter the
entertainment, the room has the function. Huge windows provide a
stunning view of the wooded area, making the room feel like an
extension of the outside space. Modern fabrics on the chaise and the
two ottomans pair well with the leather sectional and bar-height table
and chairs. During the day, light reflects off the mirror panels next to
the chaise, and at night the room feels like a chic lounge—the perfect
place to entertain. A modern painting mimics the line of the trees
beyond the white-trimmed windows, which pop against the dark
wall color.

Facing Page Top & Bottom Right: The kitchen can be the heart of a
home, especially when one welcomes and invites people to sit and
enjoy the space. Industrial pendant lights, two types of leather metallic
barstools, a copper vent, and a stainless steel commercial cooktop
make the kitchen a home chef's dream. Various types of metal, wood,
and stone were incorporated to bring nature inside. Built-in storage
features the homeowners' fine liquor collection, while another shelf
next to the stovetop houses cooking oils and sprays. The walnut island
has a built-in egg holder at the prep station. Cabinetry panels
camouflage the refrigerator and the huge island boasts
concealed storage.

Facing Page Bottom Left: Luxurious wallpaper and a quatrefoil mirror
flanked by wall sconces are the most ornate features of the bathroom.
Minimal countertop accessories keep the room uncluttered and really
allow the details—the patterns of the wallcovering, the architectural
characteristics of the mirror and the round window—to take center
stage. Flowers are a perfect accessory for bathrooms.
Photographs by Paul Konkal Photography

Searl Lamaster Howe Architects

Linda Searl fondly recalls a childhood spent gazing up at ordinary structures and imagining them as better buildings with more comprehensible designs and a greater sense of purpose. A pioneer in her field and a founding principal of Searl Lamaster Howe Architects, Linda enjoys fellowship status in the American Institute of Architects; with that prestige comes the privilege of being commissioned for the most desirable projects in the country. Along with partners Pamela Lamaster-Millett and Gregory Howe, Linda is celebrated for her architecture as well as her interior architectural designs that are at once inviting, timeless, and infused with energy.

Above & Facing Page: A multitude of windows allows for a gallery of landscapes inside the home. I pulled warm tones from the surrounding environment to optimize interior views and kept nearby decor to a minimum. The dark stair railing adds contrast to a palette of luminous hues.
Photographs by Matt Wargo

Above: Open space is essential to the homeowner who often has guests in the dining room. I used rich red fabric and soft vanilla lighting to fill the room with warmth and create an elegant atmosphere perfect for entertaining.

Facing Page: I strive to create spaces that are both modern and cozy. I enveloped the spa-like bathroom in wood paneling to maintain a sense of warmth in an otherwise chilly area. In the bedroom, rafters create a sense of intimacy while concealing the uplighting, which provides a soft glow to calm the homeowner on sleepless nights.
Photographs by Matt Wargo

"In order for a design to be successful, neither space nor materials can be wasted."
Linda Searl

Shelley Johnstone Design

While living in London, Shelley Johnstone Paschke found herself falling in love with the meticulous attention to detail the designers there embraced. Taking advantage of the good fortune of living overseas, Shelley enrolled at London's Inchbald School of Design. Early in her career, she worked with designers who inspired her to create elegant European spaces with a pared down, modern twist. Shelley starts with a solid foundation of architectural finishes and elements before adding the accents—everything from wall fabrics, ethnic prints, modern art, and mid-century modern furniture to priceless antiques—to fashion energizing, fresh spaces. With attention to detail and a pop of something unexpected in every room, Shelley's designs are engaging and timeless.

Above: I love the look of traditional patterns combined with clean lines; the fusion pays homage to the European-style elegance I love but it never feels stuffy. Bursts of color such as the orange Fortuny-style fabric and turquoise in the accessories keep the design looking young and fresh. A Greek key pattern is a traditional but fun detail that adds movement to the design but isn't overly ornate.

Facing Page: Never forget about the ceiling; an orange lacquered finish is unexpected but crowns the room perfectly. The sunburst mirror is a dynamic accent set against the trellis wall. Subtle Greek key accents on both the sofa and the light fixture help pull the room together with the rest of the home—it's important for spaces to flow from one to another. Repeating patterns or colors helps to merge all the rooms together into a cohesive environment.
Photographs by Tony Soluri

Above: Black lacquer is an easy way to dress up a staircase and gives a crisp, clean look to the surface. The foyer introduces a mix of traditional elements and unique accessories, such as the garden statue beside the table and the oversized, coral-colored, Asian-style urn.

Facing Page Top: Black lacquered cabinets and oversized, horizontally hung hardware create a masculine foundation for the kitchen. Blue and white Asian ceramics add a feminine touch, and the carrara marble countertops are absolutely timeless.

Facing Page Bottom: Two de Gournay India-inspired scenic wallpaper panels give depth to the wall behind a Greek key-adorned railing in the kitchen. French bergère-style chairs and mid-century modern coffee tables pair for a timeless design.
Photographs by Tony Soluriz

"Large-scale accents and accessories infuse a design with added interest."
Shelley Johnstone Paschke

Soucie Horner

Known for creating a rich aesthetic conducive to modern living, Soucie Horner is commissioned throughout the United States and as far away as Mexico and the UK for projects that reflect homeowners' lifestyles, whether traditional, transitional, contemporary, or modern. The residential and commercial interior architecture and design firm, led by principals Shea Soucie and Martin Horner, designs spaces with strategically planned architectural elements and well-crafted furnishings meant for real living and entertaining without a "don't touch me" attitude. The designers believe that creating a beautiful work of art is not a solitary endeavor. Rather it is the result of a collaborative process that melds owner input with professional expertise and visual sensibility. This collective effort from concept through completion is how the firm achieves remarkable interiors that are elegant, sophisticated, and always timeless.

Above: Old and new seamlessly combine for a clean traditional aesthetic. We designed classical interior architecture for the new Lincoln Park home encompassing custom millwork and finishes. An impressive Biedermeier table and baby grand piano anchor the space. Appropriate for family living, the bespoke sofa is upholstered in chenille with down pillows covered in textural vintage and contemporary fabrics. We often design architectural niches to display art: An atmospheric Chinese painting fits perfectly above our bronze-rimmed, burled walnut console fabricated by local craftsmen.

Facing Page: Architectural elements, natural materials, and custom furnishings work in harmony. The honed French limestone mantel is complemented by a hand-woven suede and linen Belgian carpet. A custom cabinet with horsehair insets discreetly houses the television. We upholstered a bergère Jacob armchair from Randolph Hein in pony hide for an air of casual elegance. The residents' rare collection of Hiro Yokose Chinese hardstone ritual blade carvings is displayed on our contrasting, clean-lined ebony étagère.
Photographs by Hedrich-Blessing, Ltd.

Above: Our clean traditional design integrated a steel window wall to permit maximum light and fresh air into the home. Industrial lighting fixtures have a refined Asian lantern vibe, casting soft beams above the antique dining table. We added an obi runner and reupholstered chairs to echo the Japanese motif. Subtle-hued walls are stippled and glazed, creating a warm backdrop for the photorealistic painting by Joseph Piccillo. We chose a hand-knotted antique Bakshaish rug to underscore the luxurious interior.

Facing Page: To enhance the urban living experience, interior architectural details must be thoughtfully planned. We designed dramatic doors with transoms that bring sunlight into the home year-round; their proportionate scale matches the grand 12-foot-high ceilings. Our minimally trimmed wall creates the perfect frame for the David Clayman painting. Traditional but with a twist, cast-bronze spindles support a hand-turned stair railing and quarter- and rift-sawn, stained oak flooring flows throughout the home. An antique Serab hallway runner softens the entry experience.
Photographs by Hedrich-Blessing, Ltd.

"Exceptional architecture is like an artist's canvas. It's the foundation on which we layer the brush strokes of design: light, color, texture, finishes, and materials."
Shea Soucie

Space Interior Design

The flow of an interior—how one room relates to the next—is a tricky thing to master, but it helps if the person steering the design is Leslie Newman Rhodes. The founder of Space Interior Design was born in New Orleans and raised there and in Europe, doodling floor plans throughout her childhood before graduating to renovating entire homes from the ground up. Her understanding of architecture, construction, and how components work together to create a fuss-free everyday home life has served Leslie well; her clientele continually rave about her creativity and management skills. Before opening Space in Chicago, she owned and co-managed a well-respected art gallery in New Orleans. Years of teaching and working in various art mediums, combined with previous experience in retail merchandising, has fueled imaginative designs while giving Leslie a healthy respect for the artisans and craftsmen who help make her plans a reality.

Above & Facing Page: The number-one element of every kitchen should be function; if it isn't easy to access things, cook on multiple appliances, clean up, and interact with others, then you'll never enjoy your kitchen no matter how beautiful it is. Low ceilings inspired me to do away with overhead cabinets and use matte glass as a backsplash to visually simplify the room. Throughout the kitchen, the cabinets are not what they seem. Although they look like drawers, they are actually large, functional cabinets. Appliances—already plugged in—pull out or ratchet up from inside the cabinets to minimize prep time and keep the owner from having to lift. All the details, including having the refrigerator handles face the same way, encourage sensible traffic patterns and keep the flow of the 50-foot-long room peaceful.
Photographs by Jorge Gera

Above: Framed artistic photographs—taken by such incredible photographers as Elliott Erwitt, Aaron Watson, Ellen Von Unwerth, and Fonville Winans, along with the work of a few family members—are the focal point of the living room. The casual display allows the collection to evolve and change over time. A neutral palette and warm wood tones complement the Chicago skyline—the transition between indoors and out isn't too jarring. White denim slipcovers are the perfect solution for high-traffic areas, since they're organic while still being tough as nails.

Right: A calm, beautiful office encourages productivity. An antique desk and Venetian chair share space with a leopard-print rug and a Fornasetti lamp found on the street. Varied textures add interest without being overwhelming.

Facing Page Top: The owner of a downtown Chicago condo wanted what she described as "transitional Zen." Light and golden colors complement a mix of furniture, letting the ever-increasing art collection take the spotlight. Furnishings are a comfortable but durable mix of high and low-price pieces.

Facing Page Bottom: I approach every room by thinking about what it might look like in ten years. That "new" shine has to age gracefully and grow with the owners, otherwise I have not done my job. The all-seasons room had to be a cozy, versatile, indoor-outdoor space. Sunbrella fabrics on the furniture and Hardie board on the walls mean that the space can survive everything from summer thunderstorms to rambunctious children. Ceiling fans, raising the roofline, and removable windows bolster the airy feeling, while heated tile floors add luxurious warmth in the winter. The enormous daybed gives the owner a comfy spot to curl up and read with her daughters, and she can seat 12 at the large family table behind the seating group.
Photographs by Jorge Gera

Susan Fredman Design Group

Susan Fredman, Barbara Ince, Aimee Nemeckay, Ruth Delf, and Sarah Davis of Susan Fredman Design Group understand the importance of connecting to the past while looking ahead to the future. The firm is grounded in the experiences and knowledge gleaned through its more than three decades in business and continues to evolve to remain vibrant and at the forefront of healthy, beautiful design. Every space celebrates the unique lifestyles, imaginations, and desires of the homeowners, and the firm's numerous designers feel rewarded as they watch the homeowners' senses of style emerge through the design process.

Above & Facing Page: The homeowners wanted their new Glencoe, Illinois, home to feel as if it had been nestled in the neighborhood for years. Carefully planned details, such as intricate mouldings, refined and rustic fireplaces, distressed finishes, custom furniture, and classic built-ins, contributed to the overall feel. The master bath and foyer are perfect examples of the sense of calm that pervades the home. Soaked by sunlight and a soft, textural palette, the bath integrates blond rift-cut oak with a champagne finish and honey onyx countertops and features his-and-hers toilet rooms, a built-in makeup table, and heated floors. The foyer is a clean space with lots of natural light that welcomes guests into the home.
Photographs by Nick Novelli, Novelli PhotoDesign

Above: The residents of a 1920s Craftsman-style bungalow love unexpected colors and wanted to weave a vibrant, saturated palette throughout the home. Bold hues and a vivid rug infuse whimsy into the library and office and provide a contrast to the traditionally shaped furniture and oak cabinetry.

Right: In the Glencoe home, the master suite foyer welcomes the homeowners to their private retreat and features intricate detailing and muted colors found throughout the rest of the space.

Facing Page Top: With insulated exterior doors and windows and heated flooring, the garden room is a luxurious space that can be used all year long for both individual leisure and intimate gatherings. Cool tones were used to complement the adjacent interior and exterior spaces.

Facing Page Bottom: An awkward, closed-off galley kitchen was transformed into a functional, bright, and spacious area fit for a chef. Three floating islands, abundant prep and storage areas, and a mix of task, cove, and pendant lighting make it a culinary enthusiast's dream.
Photographs by Nick Novelli, Novelli PhotoDesign

Sweet Peas Design

Susan Brunstrum, founder and principal designer of Sweet Peas Design, is inspired by the ideas that inspire her homeowners. She believes there is no single style that fits everyone; each person has a unique personality that should be reflected in their home. Susan and her team sculpt a project from start to finish, providing everything from floorplans and architectural drawings to remodeling the favorite room of the house. The goal is always the perfect blending of design and function; everything needs to make sense in order for homeowners and their guests to be comfortable. Utilizing different shades of the same color for a calming effect, Susan always interjects something vibrant into the palette to keep it interesting. She approaches each project with a Zen-like attitude: the process should be stress-free, designs must flow, and home should be a place for renewal.

Above: The tailored, sophisticated style I call "rough-luxe" is at play in the living room—a mingling of masculine and feminine elements in a *GQ* guy-meets-*Cosmo* girl way. The rough texture of the fireplace, which was specially painted to look like flagstone, and edginess of the glass and chrome table play off the softness of the sofas and the colorful, fashion-themed painting above the fireplace. The anchor of the room is the ivory square-in-square hide rug made by Edelman, which I designed. It pulls the pair of sofas together for an intimate conversation area.

Facing Page: For a small house, it was important to keep the design simple so I repeated colors, materials, and shapes which create continuity from room to room. In the dining room I indulged my love of circles. They repeat in the painting, the chair backs, and the crowning element in the room, the glass bead chandelier from Zia Priven. It's very glamorous and quite large—a 40-inch fixture hung over a 60-inch table—and was chosen because it fills the room.
Photographs by Jerry Kalyniuk Photography

"It's important to limit the number of 'wow' elements in a room so they don't compete for attention."
Susan Brunstrum

Above: From the silk and wool zebra rug and the sleek, blue glass accessories to the custom hand-fringed burlap fabric walls, texture is the key component in the den. The pair of chaises is critical to the room because a sofa would have consumed the space. They're perfect for watching TV, reading, and working on a laptop.

Right: A McLaughlin acrylic perching chair with long-haired goat seat makes the clear statement that the room is a woman's boudoir. Other elements are sophisticated and understated, allowing the whimsical chair to bask in the spotlight.

Facing Page Top: I try to always use creativity in seating arrangements. To make the most of a small space, I chose armless, small banquettes to flank the table and a pair of chairs. The second chair is easily pulled up from the corner for extra seating space—not all of the chairs have to be at the table at the same time.

Facing Page Bottom: The color palette for the entire house was determined by the charcoal grey cabinets and the countertop's Lumix quartzite slabs; it's a dynamite combination. The grey is tailored and soothing, while the quartzite is luxurious and exciting, like looking into a deep, clear lake. Sparkly drawer knobs that look like big engagement rings, glass pendants over the island, and stainless steel stools provide touches of shine against the cabinets' soothing backdrop.
Photographs by Jerry Kalyniuk Photography

Friese-Mier Co., page 170

Nora Schneider Interior Design, page 184

CONTEMPORARY

Jessica Lagrange Interiors, page 182

Temkin-Taylor Design, page 198

Friese-Mier Co.

Tom Friese and Robb Mier of Friese-Mier Co. believe that a room should mirror the people who live in it. Operating in Green Bay, Friese-Mier Co. has a diverse clientele developed since its founding in 1983. According to the team, who loves to share in the reward of great design with their homeowners, spaces should be artistic and individual. Pulling inspiration from owners' lifestyles, travels, and the environment that surrounds the home, Tom and Robb bring natural elements indoors, adorn walls with collected artifacts, and unabashedly mix textures to create stylish rooms for everything from entertaining to everyday life.

Above & Facing Page: A 1960s Prairie-style home designed by John Bloodgood Schuster, an architect who worked with Frank Lloyd Wright, needed some updating, but we made sure to stay true to the home's original design. The homeowners are very active in their community and wanted to extend the living space to provide more room for entertaining. Cypress beams in the ceiling and a Wright motif of arrows and triangles in the carpet pay homage to the home's roots. Panoramic windows covered by powered grasscloth Conrad shades open to the scenery beyond, and the stone hearth is constructed of local Door County ledgestone from the Niagara Escarpment. A warm, monochromatic palette provides the homeowners with an ideal space to display their art collection, and it allows their guests to add color and vibrancy to the space.
Photographs by Glen Hartjes

Above: Inspired by the homeowners' trips to Africa, the hues of the living room suggest tones associated with the continent. Framed tribal pieces collected by the owners over 25 years hang on grasscloth-covered walls. We really focused on how everything feels; blown-glass lamps and deep chocolate, caramel, and charcoal tones in the furnishings draw inspiration from the locally quarried stone fireplace.

Facing Page Top: The homeowners wanted a design that was both warm and contemporary, something that is very important in cold climates. Warmed literally and figuratively by a free-standing fireplace, the bathroom features a sleek bathtub perfect for relaxation. Locally quarried stone graces the wall behind the custom vanity with its hideaway cosmetic storage and drawer with holsters for hairdryers, curling irons, and the like. In remodeling the 1950s home, we updated the space with modern functionality.

Facing Page Bottom: Inspiration for the kitchen and dining room came from the Balinese fabric piece hung on the far wall that the homeowner acquired while traveling. Kitchen walls were torn down and the room was opened up to the rest of the living and dining area, providing the owners with plenty of space to move around and entertain. All soft furniture had to pass a touch test; velvet mohair and soft suede remain contemporary, but still comfortable and welcoming.
Photographs by Glen Hartjes

"A room is like a 3-D piece of art. As designers, we work within that art." *Tom Friese*

Above & Left: A contemporary wine cellar on the lower level of the house walks out to an enclosed sauna and hot tub, looking into the woods surrounding the home. It was very important to be able to view the wines without being inside; the walls of the cellar are enclosed in glass, aside from the portion where the television hangs.

Facing Page Top: The master bedroom and master bath combine to make the two-story master suite. Surrounded on three sides by windows, the bed faces away from the sitting area so that the view of the woods and bay below can be optimized. A resident bald eagle who likes to perch just beyond the walls is often seen from the bed. A television rises from the foot of the bed for viewing. In the sitting area, bookcases surround a fireplace, complete with a sculpture through which flames dance when lit. Birch paneling on the wall and privacy draperies on stainless steel cables offer privacy.

Facing Page Bottom: The master bathroom—located under the master suite's sitting area—includes a coffee station and stair access to the deck, which features a hot tub and an outdoor shower. Horizontal zebra veneer lines the walls of the bath and closet. A tall steam shower features floor-to-ceiling glass that looks out over the woods and the bay, but also has a privacy shade for use when desired.
Photographs by Glen Hartjes

Gooch Design Studio

Gooch Design Studio is a multidisciplinary design firm with an emphasis on the renovation and restoration of private residences, hotels, and public spaces. Its portfolio includes a rich variety of completed projects that embrace a time-honored, academic approach to design. The designers begin with a studied and collaborative process that incorporates the expectations of its clientele with the team's breadth of experience, and then continues with an informed layering of architecture, finishes, furniture, textiles, and art. Understanding the architectural requirements of a space is the foundation of the practice—the balance between sound architectural detailing and thoughtful interior design is taken very seriously, as is the opportunity to use decoration as a complementary means of providing architectural solutions. The designers rely on the continued participation of their clientele, listening closely to their needs, ideas, and ambitions to deliver an inventive solution that is uniquely their own.

Above & Facing Page: Our team worked thoughtfully to represent the homeowners' artistic sensibility in their Lincoln Park residence. While the carpet's pattern and vibrancy are playful, it was imperative that the overall design remain true to the traditional architecture of the custom limestone home. Inspired by a variety of periods and culture, the home's high levels of contrast, unusual art and accessories, custom carpets, and furniture all work to reinforce the owners' dynamic interests and taste.
Photographs by Adam Jablonski

Above & Left: Overlooking Grant Park and Monroe Harbor, the apartment is a study in contrast. The silver sofa faces a wall made entirely of windows and swathed in sheers. During the day, the room is flooded with light; at night, the floor-to-ceiling windows overlooking Lake Michigan become as black as the feature wall, dressed with a textured, woven wallcovering. Providing a balance between light and dark, the black wall also serves to separate the public and private areas of the home—something that we strive to do in many of our projects. Simple art and a custom angular console table in the entry—immediately recognizable as a reflection of the building's architecture—make for a bespoke, engaging transition from the outside world.
Photographs by Terry Manning

Facing Page: We used the homeowner's expressive fashion sense and the city's skyline as inspiration for the open penthouse loft in downtown Chicago. With a wraparound terrace and 180-degree views of the city, the home needed to be a dynamic, multifunctional space. A significant amount of engineering went into the design: the floating wall that separates the living area had to serve as a fireplace, a storage space, and a buffet for serving, and features a television on each side. It really took on a life of its own and adds so much functionality and personality to the space, without introducing a dividing wall. The room appears and feels larger by having mirrored the tray ceiling with the carpet, further reinforcing the duality of the living space.
Photographs by Terry Manning

Above & Facing Page: Elegant, refined, and monochromatic, the downtown home showcases the spectacular city views and the owners' significant art collection. As advocates for our clientele, we work with experts in other fields to expand existing art collections to suit the owners' tastes. The custom furniture is objectified against the natural silk wallcovering, which envelopes the entire apartment and creates a soft, inviting, and peaceful city residence. Ebonized wide-plank wood floors ground the space and give it polish. Usually reserved for string instruments, small flake lacewood veneer in the kitchen gives the home warmth and distinction.
Photographs by Terry Manning

Jessica Lagrange Interiors

With three-plus decades of experience in the Chicago area and throughout the country, Jessica Lagrange, principal of Jessica Lagrange Interiors, has built her reputation on designing residential interiors and pleasing the clientele who dwells within them. As her reputation suggests, Jessica's work is intricate, interesting, and polished—down to the smallest detail. With a team of experts behind the designs, homeowners' expectations are surpassed by surprisingly fresh concepts in each new project. In lieu of recycling a signature style, the firm accepts varying commissions ranging from traditional suburban habitats to contemporary city condos. The one-of-a-kind solutions have earned the designers an armoire full of awards and a wall's worth of publication covers.

Above: A modern and classic city condo offers simple style for a busy professional on the go. The homeowner wished for a clean, contemporary dining area—free from clutter—for entertaining important guests. I chose a classic series of grey, beige, cream, and taupe shades for an elegant appeal, all while employing a collection of textures from smooth to rough and shiny to matte to add interest. Contemporary wall art chosen by a fine art consultant and six Saarinen chairs make the room objectively inventive.

Facing Page: A custom-woven rug and upholstered headboard act as anchors for a vivid room dressed for a teenage girl. I applied purple hues, from the eggplant-colored wall to the fuchsia-draped bed, for drama and balanced the room with bursts of green, making a lively colorscape. An array of soft textures begs to be explored.
Photographs by Werner Straube

Nora Schneider Interior Design

Formal training and experience are imperative in the design world, but that intangible spark of innate talent is what singles out the truly great interior designers. Nora Schneider has both; she studied at Chicago's prestigious Harrington College of Design before transforming her lifelong passion for visual beauty into her own company in 1999. A champion of clean lines and the belief that a few prominent, gorgeous pieces always trump a room full of "stuff," Nora begins by pinpointing her homeowners' lifestyles and then builds her designs to accommodate their needs and wishes. Whether starting from scratch, centering a space around beloved family treasures, sourcing the perfect finishing touch, or carefully editing a room to let the showstopping pieces shine, Nora knows exactly how to achieve perfection—naturally.

Above Left: An antique music stand was the starting point for the home office, which I then augmented with the hand-sculpted and forged bronze desk by Helene Aumont and added my homeowners' collection of American and English antiques. The black leather desktop, embossed leather chair, and hair-on-hide patchwork rug add texture to the monochromatic look. The striped walls are elegant and classic yet bold, and are complemented by the Fortuny silk light fixture.
Photograph by Susan Kezon

Above Right: I love to mix the ancient and modern. As a result, the clean lines of the antique chests—used as nightstands—contrast beautifully with the bronze lamps. Resting on the bench is a Chinese headrest from the 19th century, a complement to the bamboo bed that inspired the room.
Photograph by Scott Shigley

Facing Page: The soaring, two-story space is quite interesting architecturally, which made scale and balance a challenge. From the five-foot-tall candlesticks to the red feather Bameliki headdresses scaling 15 feet up the wall, everything had to be big enough to match the scale of the space. I introduced Asian and African pieces to mix with the clean lines of the furnishings.
Photograph by Jill Buckner

"The final layer—art, artifacts, collectibles—is the most important. It's what makes a room come together." *Nora Schneider*

Above: An ancient Burmese monk's bed used as a coffee table is the focal point of the room. Surrounded by linen and leather seating and a rug made of sisal and leather, the palette is neutral enough to let the view onto Lake Geneva take center stage. Twig artwork, a collection of 19th-century Chinese headrests, and a painting stone—traditionally thought to inspire creative thoughts when placed on the desks of poets and calligraphers—add artistic interest.

Facing Page Top: The dining room is a study in rectangles, kept deliberately simple since the kitchen is located directly behind. Chinese candle stands from the late 1800s contribute a subtle glow, while a single, low-wattage light reflects the pattern of gingko leaves of the iron bowl onto the ceiling.

Facing Page Bottom: A Chinese courtyard bench is the perfect counterpoint to the brightly colored, modern abstract painting in the entryway.
Photographs by Scott Shigley

Paul Lauren Design Consultants

Inspired both by her fashion-forward mother and her early mentor Paul Marchetti, Lauren Rautbord of Paul Lauren Design Consultants has felt compelled to make the world a more beautiful place from an early age. Under Paul's wing as a teenager and then after graduating from Harrington College of Design, Lauren quickly developed her philosophy around the concept of dressing a room. She believes a room should be as well thought out as an outfit for a night on the town. Much like classic fashion icons, Lauren encourages simplicity; sometimes adding just a bit to enhance a good idea is all it takes to make it great. Whether designing a single room or an entire home, Lauren endeavors to help owners develop and improve their personal style while promoting an elegantly simple design.

Above: Light is so important in a room, and in urban spaces I believe in playing up the view. I chose low-profile furnishings to give an unobstructed view of the windows, which are adorned with shades that let the owners see out, even when lowered. Various textiles keep the space interesting and give it a luxurious feel.

Facing Page: I love combining the old and the new. Vintage leopard-print chairs pop against a neutral palette so that the room really becomes all about them. Large pieces of art and a weighted, contemporary coffee table balance out the ornate nature of the sitting area. Orange pillows add a touch of unexpected vibrancy.
Photographs by Jess Smith, PHOTOSMITH

Reddington Designs

A Chicago design mainstay since 1986, Reddington Designs balances color, texture, and scale to create sleek, sophisticated spaces. Finding the right balance between artistic minimalism and an inviting space can be a tricky endeavor, but Carol Salb and her team excel at designing contemporary homes that are both visually stunning and exceptionally comfortable. Reddington Designs brings an elevated level of inherent hospitality to contemporary living spaces through the careful placement and illumination of furnishings and artwork, and a thoughtful balance of finishes and textiles. They are experts at creating floorplans that flow easily from room to room and maximize spectacular views. Whether concealing a television behind an impressive piece of art or adding discreet, functional storage for personal items, the spaces created by Reddington Designs prove to be livable and practical in addition to being beautiful.

Above: A 2nd-century Syrian mosaic is the focal point for the wet room, which includes a whirlpool tub, steam shower, and his-and-hers rain showers, showerheads, and body spray nozzles. An additional set of interior windows was constructed to maintain the view, seal the room, and allow for maintenance of the structure's original windows. Ardhanarishvara—the deity Shiva in his half-male, half-female form—keeps watch over bathers from the bath ledge.

Facing Page: He wanted a modern, masculine, sleek concept for the living room, while she wanted the space to feel inviting, feminine, and warm. To balance these desires, we furnished the living room with subtly curved seating, luxuriant rugs, and custom lighting programs to transform the rectilinear room. Floor-to-ceiling drapery panels soften the large expanse of windows which overlook the city. One of the homeowners' favorite lighting settings is "sunrise," which allows them just enough light to sip their morning coffee on their curvy chaise as the sun emerges over Lake Michigan.
Photographs by Scott Shigley

"Good design is a balance: angular furnishings paired with warm textiles, light and shadow, masculine elements with feminine elegance." *Carol Salb*

Above: The master bedroom was deliberately designed with enough floor space for the couple to dance, practice yoga, and occasionally roll their Ping-Pong table out of the closet to play a game or two. We used sumptuous textures for the seating, bedspread, flooring, and fabric-paneled bed wall to balance the cold hardness of the floor-to-ceiling glass windows and mirrors

Right: A working home office can be beautiful as well as functional. The custom-designed eucalyptus desk, bookcase, and storage space for office supplies were built in for a clean, organized look and topped with a limestone counter replete with fossils. As an avid reader and writer, it was important for the homeowner to have her book collection at her fingertips. With frequent visits from family and friends, converting the office into a guest bedroom became a necessity. A built-in Murphy bed and slubbed silk walls create a welcoming retreat for their guests.

Facing Page Top: The deeply colored eucalyptus paneling embraces all who enter. An antique statue of Quan Yin, the goddess of mercy and compassion, creates a stunning focal point and is positioned to bless family and guests as they arrive. Flanking the statue are fresh orchids and antique, hand-painted silk panels from China.

Facing Page Bottom: Hidden behind the Tay custom paneling are moveable wall panels that divide the dining room and kitchen into two rooms. This allows the homeowner to easily shift from an open, casual plan for day-to-day living to a formal dining room with the kitchen closed off for catered events.
Photographs by Scott Shigley

Susan Fredman Design Group

Collaboration is the foundation for thoughtful, beautiful design, and Susan Fredman Design Group has been creating captivating environments using such an approach for more than 35 years. Designers Susan Fredman, Barbara Ince, Barbara Theile, Aimee Nemeckay, Terri Crittenden, Sarah Davis, and Jamie Myers believe in collaboration both between designers and homeowners and with each other to produce the best possible result. Their unique experiences and perspectives enhance the communication-rich design process and punctuate it with an unbridled enthusiasm.

Above & Facing Page: The home's angular architecture and integration with the sand, sea, and dramatic cliffs inspired us to create a personal retreat with an earthy elegance appropriate for a home perched on the edge of the Pacific. The airiness of the home combined with easy transitions and warm conversation spaces provides a striking space for entertaining. In the bedroom, a variety of textures, from nubby bouclés to supple leathers, adds visual interest and a layer of quiet sophistication next to the couple's exquisite glass, painting, and sculpture collections.
Photographs by Nick Novelli, Novelli PhotoDesign

"Comfort is physical as well as visual." *Susan Fredman*

Above: The homeowners preferred a contemporary space that was down to earth, warm, and inviting. A neutral color palette highlights the homeowners' extensive art collection and a variety of textures and materials keep the eye engaged. Soft green countertops add a hint of color and offer a natural element in the space, while glass pendants lend subtle drama. Interior flooring extends outside for a seamless transition to the patio.

Facing Page Top: In a serene downtown Chicago condo, an open layout maximizes the views and marries the interior and exterior. Subtle window treatments frame the view and can be closed for privacy.

Facing Page Bottom: In a luxurious condo, a cluttered layout was transformed into an open, contemporary space with a sleek, minimalist aesthetic. The kitchen features a juxtaposition of classic and matte soft materials. Lit glass-paneled cabinets have an interior ambient glow that functions as under-cabinet lighting, expanding the space and providing functionality, and an overhead electrical element that couldn't be moved was turned into an interesting architectural detail featuring purple heartwood.
Photographs by Nick Novelli, Novelli PhotoDesign

Temkin-Taylor Design

Design is a second career for Kim Temkin-Taylor. After 15 successful years as a clinical social worker, Kim went back to school to earn a degree in design—her passion—and she founded Temkin-Taylor Design after graduating in 2006. Applying her relationship skills and understanding of human nature to design, Kim creates spaces that grant homeowners a heightened sense of well-being. Pulling inspiration from nature, travel, fashion, and most importantly from what she learns is meaningful to homeowners, Kim knows exactly how to read between the lines and give reality to owners' ideas. Building a business on a strictly word of mouth basis, Kim's ultimate desire is to make a difference in people's lives. From participating in the Wisconsin Breast Cancer Showhouse to crafting nurturing spaces for homeowners, she not only creates beautiful rooms, but spaces that enrich lives.

Above: In the award-winning kitchen design, creating drama by balancing light and dark elements was a central concept for the cooking area. Monorail accent fixtures, uplights, and under-cabinet lighting all contribute to the illumination of the windowless area. Honed granite countertops, limestone floors, and the slate and glass mosaic backsplash provide contrast and texture to the dark custom cabinetry. Since the kitchen is very large, it had to be zoned properly to heighten functionality; there are spaces for preparation, entertaining, and casual dining. The breakfast area benefits from plenty of natural light. The space is versatile; built-in storage concealed within the window seat and a nearby task area help merge the kitchen into the rest of the room.
Photographs by Doug Edmunds Studio

Facing Page: Livable luxury was the prevailing concept for the home's entrance, which opens up to the dining and great rooms. In an open floorplan, elements such as rugs and furniture arrangements create distinct centers for activity. The cathedral ceiling, accentuated by the exposed wood trusses, is just one architectural element worth emphasizing in the room. Opposite the front door is a large picture window that overlooks a wetland conservancy. A subtle bay window in the dining room accentuates that area, while the custom stairway banister adds an organic feel to the space that is so connected to nature.
Photograph by Richard Taylor, Life Journey Photography

Tigerman McCurry Architects

Every project presents constraints, whether it is a permanent feature of the site and landscape or an element of the interior; a good architect understands how to embrace and transform those constraints into something that is purposeful and beautiful. Stanley Tigerman, FAIA, and Margaret McCurry, FAIA, have mastered this transformative skill and are known the world over for their passion for design, their embrace of alternative concepts, and their ability to create an integrated whole from sometimes disparate parts. Through their well-proportioned, elegant interpretations, the firm of Tigerman McCurry Architects creates thoughtfully conceived homes that speak to the hearts of those who reside within them.

Above & Facing Page: The incorporation of hinged partitions within the 4400-square-foot condominium provides the opportunity to either seamlessly close off discrete, private spaces or to open up the entire apartment. Through the use of timelessly elegant materials that avoid the suggestion of opulence, we accommodated the homeowner's desire for a tranquil living space, a setting suitable for entertaining on a grand scale, welcoming yet private guest quarters, and a space to display a significant contemporary art collection. And all of this was accomplished while maintaining accessibility, a prerequisite of the homeowner. *Photographs by Steve Hall, Hedrich Blessing Photographers*

Above: Situated high above Chicago's Michigan Avenue, the residence has incredible city and lake views, which we maximized through the use of an enfilade layout and a neutral color palette. Necessary structural and mechanical features transform into piers and soffits, becoming elements that showcase art and house additional lighting.

Facing Page: The entire residence imparts a sense of a classical aesthetic framed within a modernist vocabulary. This is especially evident in the master suite, where the use of elegant furnishings and monochromatic tones combines to create a contemplative, restorative atmosphere where absolutely nothing is extraneous.
Photographs by Steve Hall, Hedrich Blessing Photographers

"Every room should be well-proportioned, elegant, and capture the homeowner's aesthetic." *Margaret McCurry*

Via Design

For Valerie Schmieder and Brian Barkwell, principals at Via Design, a room is like a painting. Composition, color, texture, rhythm, and positive and negative space play a role in each art form and, like great masterpieces, Via Design's spaces endure through both trends and time. Merging mid-century modern furniture with current pieces, mixing an array of textures—from hand-woven rugs to chrome bocce ball lights that rain down a stairwell—spaces created by the multi-disciplinary design team focus on the lifestyle of homeowners. The eclectic yet undeniably comfortable living spaces are the result of sculptural design utilizing materials and space as a medium.

Above Left: A floating sculptural fireplace separates the living and dining spaces in the urban condominium. Open spaces created in the historic building prove to be adaptive reuses for modern living, accommodating intimate spaces as well as flexible entertaining for large groups. A mix of materials, including polished granite, cerused walnut, hand-blown glass, natural wool rugs, and stainless surfaces, are contrasted against a simple white canvas.

Above Right: A cantilevered sculptural staircase connects the seventh-floor living space to a penthouse entertaining floor, providing panoramic views of the city. Mid-century modern furniture contrasts with a concrete, glass, and stainless custom stairway in the dynamic two-story space. Touches of persimmon add contrast and excitement to the otherwise neutral palette.

Facing Page: The original rooftop of the historic building was converted into a penthouse entertaining area, blending indoor and outdoor spaces through the use of retractable glass walls. An outdoor lounge area was created adjacent to green rooftop sculpture gardens, and an upper level viewing platform was added to offer 360-degree views of the sweeping landscapes and wandering river.
Photographs by Brian Kelly

index

Morgante-Wilson Architects, page 128

INTERIORS

MIDWEST TEAM

ASSOCIATE PUBLISHER: Terri Mankus

GRAPHIC DESIGNER: Jen Ray

EDITOR: Megan Winkler

MANAGING PRODUCTION COORDINATOR: Kristy Randall

HEADQUARTERS TEAM

PUBLISHER: Brian G. Carabet

PUBLISHER: John A. Shand

ART DIRECTOR: Emily A. Kattan

GRAPHIC DESIGNER: Lauren Schneider

MANAGING EDITOR: Lindsey Wilson

EDITOR: Alicia Berger

EDITOR: Nicole Pearce

TRAFFIC SUPERVISOR: Drea Williams

DEVELOPMENT & DISTRIBUTION SPECIALIST: Rosalie Z. Wilson

ADMINISTRATIVE COORDINATOR: Amanda Mathers

ADMINISTRATIVE ASSISTANT: Aubrey Grunewald

PANACHE PARTNERS, LLC
CORPORATE HEADQUARTERS
1424 Gables Court
Plano, TX 75075
469.246.6060
www.panache.com

Kathleen Newhouse, page 34

Space Interior Design, page 156

THE PANACHE COLLECTION

CREATING SPECTACULAR PUBLICATIONS FOR DISCERNING READERS

Dream Homes Series

An Exclusive Showcase of the
Finest Architects, Designers and Builders

Carolinas
Chicago
Coastal California
Colorado
Deserts
Florida
Georgia
Los Angeles
Metro New York
Michigan
Minnesota
New England

New Jersey
Northern California
Ohio & Pennsylvania
Pacific Northwest
Philadelphia
South Florida
Southwest
Tennessee
Texas
Washington, D.C.

Spectacular Homes Series

An Exclusive Showcase of the Finest Interior Designers

California
Carolinas
Chicago
Colorado
Florida
Georgia
Heartland
London
Michigan
Minnesota
New England

Metro New York
Ohio & Pennsylvania
Pacific Northwest
Philadelphia
South Florida
Southwest
Tennessee
Texas
Toronto
Washington, D.C.
Western Canada

Perspectives on Design Series

Design Philosophies Expressed
by Leading Professionals

California
Carolinas
Chicago
Colorado
Florida
Georgia
Great Lakes
London

Minnesota
New England
New York
Pacific Northwest
South Florida
Southwest
Toronto
Western Canada

Art of Celebration Series

Inspiration and Ideas from
Top Event Professionals

Chicago & the Greater Midwest
Colorado
Georgia
New England
New York
Northern California
South Florida
Southern California
Southern Style
Southwest
Toronto
Washington, D.C.

City by Design Series

An Architectural Perspective

Atlanta
Charlotte
Chicago
Dallas
Denver
New York
Orlando
Phoenix
San Francisco
Texas

Spectacular Wineries Series

A Captivating Tour of Established,
Estate and Boutique Wineries

California's Central Coast
Napa Valley
New York
Ontario
Sonoma County
Texas
Washington

Experience Series

The Most Interesting Attractions,
Hotels, Restaurants, and Shops

Austin & the Hill Country
Boston
British Columbia
Chicago
Southern California
Twin Cities

Interiors Series

Leading Designers Reveal Their Most Brilliant Spaces

Florida
Midwest
New York
Southeast
Washington, D.C.

Spectacular Golf Series

The Most Scenic and Challenging Golf Holes

Arizona
Colorado
Ontario
Pacific Northwest
Southeast
Texas
Western Canada

Weddings Series

Captivating Destinations and Exceptional Resources
Introduced by the Finest Event Planners

Southern California

Specialty Titles

The Finest in Unique Luxury Lifestyle Publications

21st Century Homes
Cloth and Culture: Couture Creations of Ruth E. Funk
Distinguished Inns of North America
Dolls Etcetera
Extraordinary Homes California
Geoffrey Bradfield Ex Arte
Into the Earth: A Wine Cave Renaissance
Luxurious Interiors
Napa Valley Iconic Wineries
Shades of Green Tennessee
Spectacular Hotels
Spectacular Restaurants of Texas
Visions of Design

Panache Books App

Inspiration at Your Fingertips

Download the Panache
Books app in the iTunes
Store to access select
Panache Partners
publications. Each book
offers inspiration at your
fingertips.

Panache Partners, LLC   1424 Gables Court   Plano, Texas 75075   469.246.6060   www.panache.com